CLAUDE AND HIS BUS

AN ADVENTURE ON EVERY TRIP

Claude Boucher

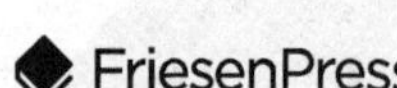

One Printers Way
Altona, MB R0G 0B0
Canada

www.friesenpress.com

First Edition — 2023

Editor– Jessica Ruston

ISBN
978-1-03-917931-8 (Hardcover)
978-1-03-917930-1 (Paperback)
978-1-03-917932-5 (eBook)

1. TRANSPORTATION, PUBLIC TRANSPORTATION

Distributed to the trade by The Ingram Book Company

Milas, (Modern Auto Tech).

It's Truly My Pleasure To Be Able To Share My Book With You!

Both You And Mike Are Excellent Role Models For Which My Book Is Intended! You Both Care!

Many Thanks! Claude.

"A feel-good book in troubled times - an interpersonal look at the relationship between a bus driver and passengers."

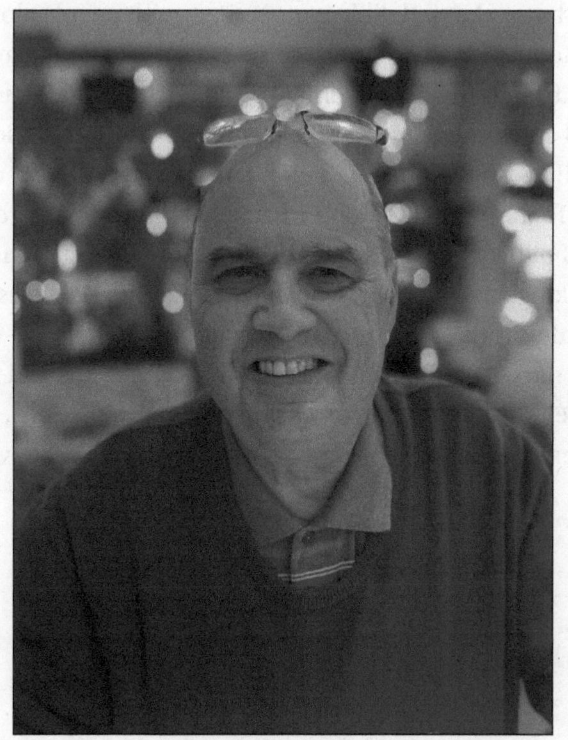

(Claude Boucher) (Picture by Genevieve Roy)

Mar 2024

About - by Jessica Ruston

The little interactions we have in life impact us in ways that we might not understand in the moment. Our journey takes on all sorts of paths and routes. These routes represent those magical moments in life that affect us forever. Come along on the journey of a man who not only takes these routes daily but makes indelible connections with people along the way.

Claude Boucher is the quintessential every-man. Protector of family and loyal to friends, he has never let the adversities of life dull his spirit. Able to read and understand people in a way that only a seasoned expert in all that life – the good and bad – has to offer, Claude connects to people and forges a unique bond that only a few people are capable of producing. Follow along as he shares his unique interactions in a vastly diverse working environment. Chronicling his experience as a GTA bus driver, Claude captures moments that will change how we think about people, and ourselves. Take a seat at the front of the bus and witness to a journey of self-awareness, ways to navigate tough situations, and how to always remember that one must taste the sour to enjoy the sweet.

Dedication - by Jessica Ruston

Never has someone been so lucky to be a Pappy to five amazing grandchildren. Wherever you go in life, lead with compassion and love. Work hard and the rest will fall into place. Remember that no matter where Pappy is, he will always be with you on your journey.

To Lucas, Malia, Gabriel, Elias, and Sebastian; Pappy loves you, always and forever.

A Special Tribute - by Claude Boucher

If it were not for my daughter Danielle Boucher and a very dear friend Connie Rizzo, this book may have never happened. You see, both Danielle and Connie are remarkable teachers, and we were exchanging stories of events in their classrooms and on my bus. They loved my stories and suggested I write them down for posterity for my grandchildren. Given all the negativity we are dealing with daily, I felt it was an awesome idea and suggestion. As such, my heartfelt thank you to both Danielle and Connie... you "started my bus!"

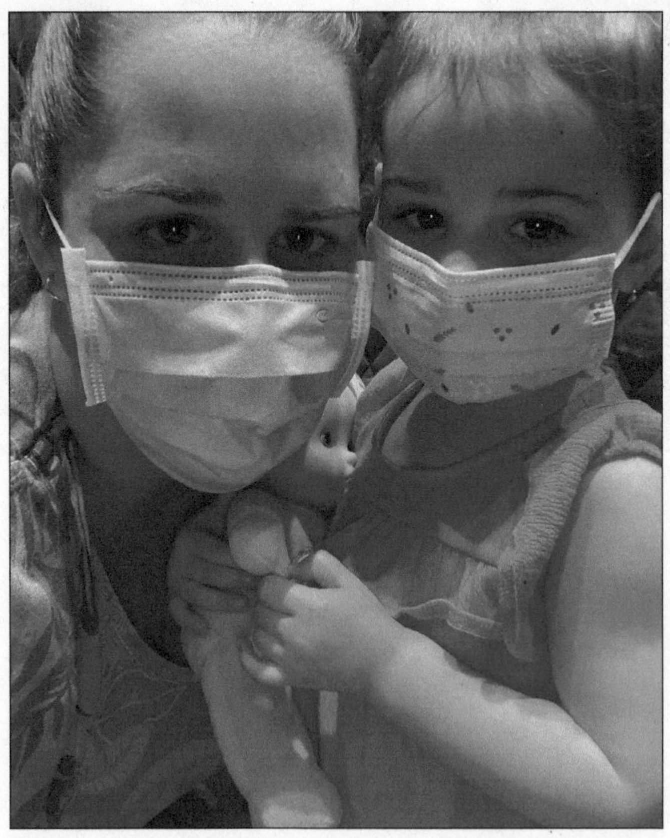

Testimonials

Lisa Haley

(Head Coach - During my days driving "Coach-Buses," specifically for the Ryerson University Women's Hockey Team... prior to driving Urban Transit Buses.)

Riding on a bus from city to city is just a routine part of the job that I do. Except it hardly feels like a job. It feels more like a way of life. I have been a professional hockey coach for 25 years. That is a lot of road trips; a lot of hours sitting in the right-hand seats in the front row of a charter bus, watching the lines of the pavement dash by, killing time on the bus until we get to our next destination. Bus drivers come and go, weekend after weekend, some are cranky old 'you know what's', others are young and keen, but honestly scary as heck behind the wheel in bad weather. Some are super chatty, completely oblivious that I might be fully exhausted and just want to sleep, as they ramble on with their chatter.

Flipping the calendar back to the early 2012's, I had just taken a new coaching job at Ryerson University. That meant moving my young family from small town Nova Scotia to the largest city in Canada. And to a hockey program that did not exist before I came. We were starting from scratch. We had just finished our first full season as a team, and our record was 1-22-1. That is a lot of losses, and a lot of LONG bus rides home afterwards. It was a lot of young women trying to find their way and their self-confidence. Tough when you are getting the pants beat off you every game and doubting if you are good enough to be in this league.

Then, this one road trip we met Claude. He was such a breath of fresh air. It took him no time at all to know every single player and coach by name. He quickly knew all about each of us, really connecting with us as people. As friends. I wasted no time in requesting Claude for every possible road trip we could for the rest of that season. He was not just a bus driver to us. He was a friend, a confidante, a father figure to the players, and a coaching colleague of mine as he shared his own experiences as a sports coach. He was our protector, our sounding board, our 'picker-upper' when we got blown out in a game. He was our biggest fan, he was inspirational, he was motivating, he was empathetic, he was exactly what we needed when we did not even know we needed it. Claude is the guardian angel over your shoulder. He just happens to come into your life because he drives a bus.

It has been a decade since Claude spent that hockey season with us, driving us all over Ontario in the best and worst weather Mother Nature could send our way. But it is not those moments that stick out. It is the true friendship from Claude that we all cherish. To this day, over 10 years later, he is a part of our lives. Over our shoulders cheering us on, offering congrats as each player gets married, has kids, graduates from Vet school, or letting us know he is there when we lose a loved one.

I vividly remember Claude once dropping our team off at the Mattamy athletic Centre, then driving me home right to my door to make sure I got home safe. Who does that!? I remember the weather being so awful we could not get up the little hill at Keele Street in Toronto and he kept everyone so calm and patient as he found another way.

I have always tried to teach my players and my kids that if you live life the right way, that if you do the right thing, take the high road, show people respect, that you will live a life full of meaning and fulfillment. I want my teams to 'win the right way.' This is what Claude does, he lives the right way. That is what I admire most about him. Claude helps people reach their best potential. This is a gift he has been blessed with.

Claude, you have made so many lives just a little bit brighter. Every player and coach from that Ryerson team a decade ago loves and cares for you, because of the love and care you showed for us. I am so fortunate to have met such a wonderful human being, and it is a privilege to offer this small message to you for your book.

Thank you, my friend.

Lisa Haley

Head coach, TMU Hockey, Senior VP of hockey operation, PHF.

TMU - Toronto Metropolitan University.

PHF - Premier Hockey Federation

Assistant Coach Sochi 2014 – Winter Olympics in Russia

Melissa Wronzberg

(Player - Also, during my days driving "Coach-Buses," and specifically for the Ryerson University Women's Hockey Team...)

17 minutes. According to Google maps, that is about how long it would take for me to walk from my home at Gerard and Parliament to the Mattamy Athletic Centre. At this point, I was in my second year at the former Ryerson University, studying Journalism and competing for the women's hockey team. It has been a long time, about 10 years in fact, but I will never forget being introduced to our bus driver, Claude, 'like close the door' Boucher. Not only did he make an impact on each of us, but he also changed my routine that season.

Many hockey players have superstitions or routines, and I was no different. I had my route that I would walk to the rink each day for games and practices, but one day that changed. It was maybe just the second or third time Claude was going to be driving our team bus. As I started on my walk to the arena I noticed a Canada coach bus on the side of the road, I thought nothing of it until I heard someone holler at me. It was Claude, of course. He asked me how I was doing and if I was headed to the rink. Being the nice man he is, he then offered if I wanted to hop on the bus and he would give me a ride instead of having to walk. I did not know Claude well, yet, but I guess I felt comfortable enough to accept the ride. I never minded the walk to the rink. It was time for me to clear my head and get some fresh air, it was not that long of a walk for me either seeing as I did it daily, but Claude was kind enough to offer, and I was not going to say no. This became my new pregame routine before every road trip. As our coach requested Claude for all our away games, he made it his routine to wait for me to get on the bus by my house and drive me to the rink. It was like I had my own personal chauffeur!

This is only a piece of how kind and caring Claude is. I always will remember the time I DID NOT meet up with Claude for our pregame routine. He had given me a ride several times already, but one game day I headed to the rink early to get some Athletic Therapy treatment. Claude and I never exchanged phone numbers, so I had no way to give him the heads up that I would not be at our normal spot at our normal time.

When I walked on the bus outside of the arena that day, I remember seeing the look of relief that came across Claude's face and him asking where I had been. He told me he waited for me as long as he felt he could before he headed to the rink and was worried about where I was. This was just one example of how much Claude cared for not just me, but every member of our team.

These bus rides, just Claude and I, was a nice way for us to get to know each other more. He was not just the bus driver; he became a part of the team. Not only did the staff and players get to know him, but my parents and others did too. I have been on a lot of team buses after five years of university, two years in the pros, and now a few years as a coach. Most bus drivers drop the team at the rink and then leave, but not Claude. Claude was our biggest fan, sticking around and cheering us on at games. He supported every player and knew what to say, even when we thought we did not deserve any compliments, Claude was handing them out.

Unfortunately, Claude couldn't be our bus driver forever. Even if we tried to fight for it. But that was not going to stop Claude from still being part of our team. Claude still went out of his way after he was no longer our bus driver to make sure he got to one of our games, even the way in Kingston! Claude knew that meant a lot to us, and if he did not, it definitely showed when I told my parents they had to wait while I went to say hi to Claude first when I noticed him sticking around waiting to greet us.

To this day, Claude shows up for members of that team he drove the bus for. He tags us on Facebook in fun or encouraging posts, sends us messages of happy holidays, birthdays, and congrats when it is fitting. Sometimes, he just checks in on our lives from time to time and updates us on his own.

I have always enjoyed hearing Claude's stories of his bus driving adventures. I felt special because he took some extra time out of his day to wait for me and give me a ride to the rink each day. The best part is knowing the type of person he is, that he would and does things like this for anyone that comes across his path. By nature, Clause is a caring and giving individual, and these stories amplify those characteristics.

If everyone in the world showed a little bit of the empathy that Claude does, this world would be a far greater place.

Melissa Wronzberg

Claude Boucher #1 fan

Sales Rep Athletic Knit

Former Professional Hockey Player – Markham Thunder

Current Coach – Leaside Wildcats Women's Hockey

Mike Nixon

(Lieutenant – Sea Cadets / Also, during my "Coach" Bus driving days prior to driving Urban Transit.)

I have been involved with the Canadian Cadet Organization since joining as a sea cadet in 1971 and have been fortunate to have travelled across Canada and the United States. All this travel wasn't exclusively by bus, but it was inevitable that a bus would be used to transport us. Of all the bus trips I have been on, I can only remember one driver.

I first met Claude on 8 June 2012. He was the driver for our trip to attend Rendezvous Naval 2012 being conducted in Quebec City, PQ. 8-11 June 2012. We started off in CFB Borden at 7:15 am with stops in Newmarket, Toronto, Ajax, Cornwall, and arriving in Quebec City at 7:30 pm. All of us were immediately impressed with Claude's calmness and sense of humour. Over the next few days, he was a constant source of reliability and provided some very sage advice about the city and its most interesting features.

Needless to say, it has been almost ten years since we met, and I still follow his exploits through Facebook. Claude's act of kindness towards those who are facing challenges is heartwarming and has occasionally caused small liquid droplets to form at the corner of my eyes. I truly believe that most people are good but if more were like Claude the world would be a far better place.

Bien joué mon ami,

Salutations,

Lt(N)/ Ltv Michael K Nixon

J5 Plans Officer (Sea Cadets) - Regional Cadet Support Unit (Central) Canadian Armed Forces
J5 Officier des plans (Cadets de la Marine) - Unité régional de soutien aux cadets (Centre) Forces armées canadiennes

(A gift from the kids of the Sea Cadets)

Paul Crosby - (Supervisor)

It takes an exceptional person of character to turn a mundane job into an endless opportunity to serve people with kindness and compassion. I have been in the transit industry for 22 years, as a driver, supervisor, and controller. I have worked in three of Canada's biggest transit systems including Winnipeg, Vancouver, and Mississauga, and I have never met anyone as committed to excellence, with no other reward than internal satisfaction, as Claude Boucher.

Not only does Claude perfectly model established corporate values of trust, quality, and excellence, but he continuously goes far above and beyond any call of duty to touch lives with infectious positivity and genuine caring.

Claude's stories will change your opinions about how everyday public servants can have a dramatic impact and leave a lasting legacy. They will provide a glimpse into the soul of an extremely rare breed of modern worker, and you will come away thrilled, and possibly desiring to be a transit operator.

It has been an honour and a privilege to work side by side with Claude. If all operators approached their job this way, I probably wouldn't have a job!

Paul Crosby

Control and Route Supervisor

Urban Transit

Janice Camilleri - (Supervisor)

I have been in the transportation industry for 27 years and have encountered many individuals in my travels. None however shine as brightly as Claude Boucher. He emits positivity wherever he goes and isn't afraid to express his feelings of gratitude for life and love. He leaves a path of warmth and kindness that leaves one feeling uplifted.

My first encounter as a supervisor attending to his bus left me in awe of Claude. He had identified an individual that had been reported missing by the police. When I arrived at his bus, he was sitting with the gentleman speaking calmly and showing him pictures of his beloved grand children. Never has there been such a prouder Pappy. Claude identified the need of this individual and went out of his way to help him, resulting in the gentleman being reunited with his family.

Claude is a pillar within the transit community, and I feel privileged to know him and work with him.

Janice Camilleri
Control and Route Supervisor
Urban Transit

Sebastian Valvo – (Trainer)

I have had the honor of meeting many special and talented people in my 22 years as a Training Officer. However, few come close to leaving a lasting impression like Claude did. Being a professional Transit Operator demands many qualities that few individuals have the capability to demonstrate on a daily basis.

Claude is one of those few individuals that exemplifies the role of a Transit Operator on every level. Not only is Claude a skilled driver, but he is also capable of empathy and compassion on a level that transcends Customer Service. He makes each customer feel like they are a friend, and that is priceless.

I wish I understood cloning better because I would make a warehouse full of Claude's! But alas, there is only one Claude, and he is priceless. And we are overjoyed to have him on our team.

Sebastian Valvo
Trainer, Urban Transit

Steve Roberts – (Supervisor / Peer Trainer)

I have been in Urban Transit for 16 years. Most of which was as an operator/bus driver until my advancement as a Route Supervisor for the past three years. Along the way I have met many individuals which make me proud to be associated with the type of people who become bus drivers.

The makeup of a good bus driver is very diverse and complex, but what stands out in my opinion is one's common sense and obsession with safety and customer service. We do not transport cargo; we move family members who are going about their daily routines with the intent of going home at the end of their day.

It takes a special person to be a bus driver and when I was selected as Claude's Peer trainer, I felt so encouraged by his amiable and caring nature. I simply that I knew we had a keeper on our hands, as his driving skills were obvious.

Claude was an absolute pleasure to train, and in fact over the years I have learned from Claude how to be more positive and empathetic as the rigors of what we do day in, and day out can take an incredible toll on us. Do not ever change young fella and please, continue giving our passengers the best of what you do! Truth be told, you are truly special.

Steve Roberts
Route Supervisor
Previous Peer Trainer
Urban Transit

Rafi Ebraemi – (Peer / Executive Union Representative)

Urban Transit has been my home away from home for over 20 years now. I started as a junior driver when I was in my early 20's and always looked forward to the daily camaraderie with my fellow drivers, superiors, and customers. Working for our company has always fostered a true sense of community and family for myself and many other drivers.

When Claude joined the team, we immediately developed a true sense of mutual understanding and appreciation. When I began working my way through the chain of command and joined the transit union in an official position, we furthered our alliance and friendship. He has always taken the time out of his busy schedule to check-in with me; "how was your weekend/day? And how is the family"? If I had any questions or required support, he was always available and supportive. Having a colleague that genuinely cares and has your best interest at heart is most definitely an amazing experience and benefit to working with Claude. Notwithstanding his experience in Management, and as a former Union Steward prior to his days as a Transit Operator.

Claude truly embodies the qualities our company fosters in their work environment and our team is very fortunate to have Claude as an employee. Our passengers/customers that travel on his bus routes, also benefit from his daily care, consideration, and humour.

Thank you, Claude, for being you!

Rafi

ATU Executive Board Member

Transit Operator

Urban Transit

Jack Jackson - (Executive Union President)

I have been with transit for a little over 20 years. When you work this long in transit it often feels like living a separate life with a large extended family because of the hours we keep. In this separate work life, I have been privileged enough to enjoy the pleasure of working with so many amazing people during the two plus decades of employment.

During this time, I have had the privilege of working alongside Claude. Claude is someone who continues to challenge all those around him to be a better person in every way possible. Claude has a unique way of looking at the role of a transit operator while ensuring that the public has always remained his top priority. A priority that ensures his passengers are safe, cared for and most of all, shown the respect that they deserve. He has always had the ability to deal with the everyday grind while taking the time to lend an ear, an infectious smile, and the odd quip with those who ride his bus.

If you want to be entertained while being intellectually challenged, then you simply need to look no further than a Claude Boucher conversation!

Jack Jackson

ATU Union President

Urban Transit

Sharmishta Gosh – (Passenger)

It was three years ago when I was new to Canada, and I was travelling to meet with my Immigration Lawyers. With a lot of things going on in my life from immigration paperwork to settling in new country, I was totally lost. In fact, even on this day I was unsure of the bus route and was extremely vulnerable and lost. That's when I discovered Claude who came to my rescue and helped me reach my destination.

Claude was proactive, kind, and humble, and he really understood my situation. Not only did he drop me at my destination on that day, but also told me how to get home. He let me keep in touch on social media realizing that I am new and might need some guidance. Ever since that day, I've had a friend, a father figure, and a mentor / guide to go to for anything depending on my situation. He always came forward to help / guide me in my pursuit of life. He is always there to console me / guide me or direct me to right things in life when I feel lost. He is always and will always be my go-to person especially after my father died. He gave me comfort and came as a great human being. I really appreciate his presence in my life and am very happy to have him as my friend and a mentor.

One Bus ride and I found a great person in him who always stands by me. We don't need to change the whole world, but instead we need to change and be more like Claude - humble, kind, gracious, and forgiving. Believe me, this world would be a great place to live. Thank you, Claude, for the bus ride on that day and for still being here for me. I wish you a very healthy and amazing life. I just hope that you always know that you have me at your back. Thank you once again, and I just want to say you are a very beautiful and amazing person.

Sharmishta Gosh

A grateful passenger and aspiring Canadian from Kolkata, India

Contents

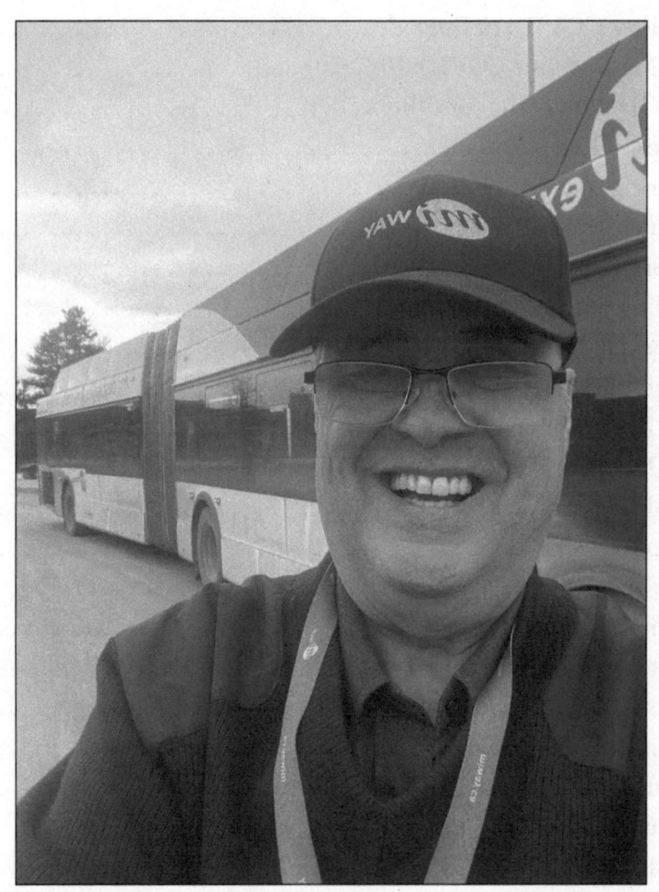

(Claude Boucher)

Chapter 1

What makes a good bus driver...

YOU KNOW, DRIVING A BUS IS SO COMPLEX YET SO SIMPLE. Folks look at us sitting on our butts and merely driving. Nice, eh? Well, from my perspective it takes many qualities and skills. In my view, the underlying qualities are empathy and compassion. Driving is the easy part of operating an Urban Transit bus. It is everything else which puts us on trial every single trip.

In a split-second, things can go from being very pleasant to seriously tense, and not because of the weather or traffic conditions. You know the adage of the 90 - 10 factor? In that, life is 10% what happens in our lives and 90% is how we react to those things. React negatively and it grows, react positively and it dissipates as it is deescalated.

As drivers our buttons are pushed time and time again. What always stands out, for me anyway, is the "why?"

So much can happen in the blink of an eye, but it is composure and compassion which keeps me going. It is also very true that I love my job. Driving is the easy part, no matter the driving conditions. Be it traffic or weather, it is all of the other stuff which needs constant attention and reinforcement.

Yesterday everything was going along oh so smoothly, when I approached a bus stop with about six people waiting for me. Once they boarded, a young couple in their mid-twenties came from behind the glass shelter with two grocery bags each. Right away I thought, "why the delay, didn't they see me coming, why wait until the last moment to begin moving to board the bus?" Anyway, they are now on, and the fellow is looking at her to pay. She puts her bags down and begins going through her little change pouch. As she does, I noticed the ragged clothing they were wearing, and that it wasn't groceries in the bags but possessions. Things like crumpled up clothing and an alarm clock.

She finally puts in the fare for both, but with not enough to even cover half the cost of a single fare. Reading into the situation I said, "no worries" as the look in her eyes was that of 'please don't be angry' I looked at her partner and his look said, 'please'! My heart melted as I noticed a baby bump.

The struggles some face in silence is truly amazing. This young couple looked to me to be new immigrants who somehow managed to get to a country for a new and better life, and here they were finding out things are not so ideal. They graciously accepted the two transfers I handed them, and their smiles were of mixed gratitude and embarrassment. I could not help but notice, as they sat near the front in my sightline, they never said a word or looked at each other. They sat with their heads down as though in a trance merely gazing at the floor.

I could not help but feel the stress and pressures of their life. I vividly remember seeing my mother exhibit similar types of stress and pressure time and time again. She was trying to raise nine children in slums, and then in a luxury townhome of a subsidized housing project while on welfare.

We travelled about 15 stops, and I thought about what I might be able to do for them. My hands felt tied as I am a mere bus driver, and my options are extremely limited given my position and situation. My primary duty is to get folks from point A to point B in a safe and timely manner. Well, I simply could not leave it at that as my heartstrings kept telling me to do something.

They pulled the stop cord and I had to act fast. So, I quickly reached into my pocket and grabbed all the money from my pocket and folded it into a transfer. As they exited the back door and began walking by the front door, I opened it and called them over. Both were very confused, as I had to open my protective shield, lower my mask and while smiling motion for them to come back. As she did, I secretly handed her the folded transfer and said, "for your baby."

The look on her face was confusion. She got off the bus and began opening the transfer and saw the money. At first, they both had incredible smiles, which I saw for the first time as their faces lit up. Then the woman began crying. I put a finger over my mouth to try and tell her it was ok as I waved goodbye. My God, I could feel the tears welling in my eyes, but I had to stay focused.

I managed to keep it together. About four stops later, an old man I have seen many times before with his distinctive Turban exited the bus. He walked to my front doors and asked me to open them. As I did, he looked me in the eye and put his hands together as in prayer with a huge smile. I thought he must have witnessed what happened earlier with the young couple and was thanking me. Oh boy, the tears began again. What an incredible feeling he bestowed on me. I smiled while reciprocating his gesture and closed the doors to continue on my way.

I know all bus drivers are not like me. What I have learned is that my life experiences are unique to me, as we are all unique. But we all have it within us to be kind and compassionate. Sure, we can all slip into dwelling on the negative side of the 10% that we are faced with. But, by simply being aware of it we can work on staying positive.

A little kindness goes a long way in our own well-being.

Chapter 2

Priceless Memories...

I'M GOING TO GO A BIT OFF TOPIC HERE AS A BIT OF BACK-ground into me as it may give you some insights into my character. I'm extremely diverse in my interests and in the past got bored doing redundant repetitive jobs. Operating a Bus is so extremely diverse with all its requirements, despite it appearing very routine. I feel these diverse experiences paved the way for me!

Born in Montreal, Les Canadiens (the Habs) were my favourite NHL hockey team. Then in 1961 or 1962, we moved to Toronto... I remained a Habs fan.

Then, in 1963 my father took me to Maple Leaf Gardens to see a Toronto Marlies game. We got there early, and I was simply in awe of everything about the place. It was magical and awe inspiring!

Our seats were way up in the Greys, but as we walked into the seating area we walked through a tunnel of sorts, and the skies opened in my eyes. This, surely, was heaven.

That bright silver ceiling, the huge clocks at the ends with a huge picture of the Queen, and that beautiful Blue Maple Leaf at Centre Ice!

The ice shimmered in white with beautiful white boards surrounding the ice rink. It was a sight which stole my heart.

It was at that point my father had inadvertently converted me into a Toronto Maple Leaf fan! When we were in the hallway, he told me all the names of the great players pictured on the walls. I learned more about those great Toronto players than my father took for granted. I knew of the great Montreal Players we had left in Montreal.

Later in my childhood I even got to play 2 Hockey Championship games there and did not allow a single goal. Back then there were no Goalie awards, but in our second Championship, the Coaches from our league all chipped in to buy me a plaque with a picture of a Goaltender on it. Trust me, we had a powerhouse team with fellow players such as Jim Kaludis and Archie King, so my work was limited.

Years later I was with the Ice Follies (similar to Disney on Ice), one year as HR Pufnstuf, and the following year as Mayor McCheese. I was too young to travel so I only did the shows in Toronto. What an incredible experience. I even got to ride the Zamboni during intermissions. Scraping and cleaning the ice during Toronto Maple Leaf games with the Hamburglar standing on the blade section while I was sitting on a top corner close to the driver. Both in costume, of course.

In fact, during one intermission my (Mayor McCheese's) hat fell off while we were cleaning the ice on our final run down the middle. Inside the head was a helmet, but one of the bands was broken which secured the head. So, for the head to look straight I had to hold my head on an angle. My neck was absolutely killing me, and I straightened up figuring the fans would just think I was making a funny gesture. Suddenly, the fans started laughing and clapping. I asked the driver what was going on. His exact words were, "your f**king hat fell off right on our Maple Leaf and I'm going to have a damn hard time getting it off now!"

About 10-15 years later I was an Usher in Maple Leaf Gardens ending up in the Press Box in the Gondola. This is where injured or retired players often sat. I got to meet some greats; my idol Johnny Bower, Bobby Baun, Gordie Howe, Bobby Orr, Bobby Hull etc., I could go on and on.

Then later in life I had the rare honour of being the bus driver of the Ryerson Rams University women's hockey team coached by Lisa

Haley. There were notable players like Melissa Wronzberg and Jessica Hartwick, just too many to list. It was like they became my kids. They were just an incredible group of beautiful people. You may not be aware, but the old Maple Leaf Gardens is now home to the Ryerson Rams (now the Toronto Metropolitan University after its name changed), and in fact the ceiling is the same and I can see where my old perch was.

Well, in my heart I am a Toronto Maple Leaf fan first, but it seems my first love (the Habs) are always there to console me, or at the very least to keep me in line as my Leafs continue to toy with my heart with their losing ways.

Again, having our hopes dashed, it's Go Habs Go (as my Leafs have been once again eliminated). As for my Leafs... well, just wait for next year...lol!

Chapter 3

Old Man Leaving His Temple...

IT WAS IMPOSSIBLE NOT TO NOTICE AN OLDER GENTLEman leaving a Temple while on my evening bus route. He was wearing an old and weathered coat, tethered pants, and worn-out shoes about three or four sizes too big for his feet. All of this told its own story in my mind; one of struggle, hard times, and someone just trying to get by. As he boarded the bus, I covered the opening to the collection box, ensuring that this gentleman did not need to use his Loonie for the bus ride. It was then that his eyes revealed a truly thoughtful sentiment; one of humble gratitude and appreciation. As he exited the bus, he gently touched my shoulder and smiled. This kind gesture left me thinking of how truly fortunate I am. After all, we all have struggles, I am so glad I have mine and not his. They teach us a lot about life. Especially how all it takes is a little kindness to feel great inside.

Chapter 4

Thank You...

IT WAS CERTAINLY NICE TO HAVE A FEEL GOOD EVENT ON my route after a weekend off. For my passengers, that might be quite old, have a walker, or show signs of a disability, I try to help them out as much as I can. During inclement weather or under certain conditions, I will drop them off in the safest location in relation to their destination. For frequent passengers, sometimes they do not even need to make the request – I will simply help them out.

Today, I dropped off an older man at his apartment's driveway. Traffic was congested, and I remembered him, so it worked out well. Before exiting, he gently tapped my leg. Assuming this was his 'thank you', I started to exit the entrance to his driveway. Then, I felt something on my leg. Low and behold, it was a banana wrapped in a paper towel! While a simple 'thank you' would suffice, this man meticulously chose this banana for me. After years of working in my brother's Tropical fruit and grocery store, I know a good banana when I see one - lol! The banana was perfect; not too ripe and not too large! But his expression of gratitude... his 'thank you' - was a wonderful yet simple act of kindness which truly touched me!

Chapter 5

Mixed Emotions...

NOTHING QUITE LIKE A FEEL-GOOD MOMENT SHROUDED with mixed emotions. A woman, who did not appear to be a Senior (in her mid 40's), began to put a Senior's ticket (which costs $2) into the fare box. I stopped her, as the Senior's fare is $1 after 7:30pm. Confused, she looked at me wondering what was happening. I tried to explain the fare structure to her, and she looked even more confused. I soon realized she was deaf and began making inaudible sounds to try and communicate with me. I began to explain the fare amount to her. Using simple hand signs, and verbalizing words with my mouth in the hopes she might be able to read my lips, but this did not work. I even pointed to the fare rates on the bus display panel, but that did not quite work either. Finally, I exempted her fare and handed her a transfer.

The woman went and sat down. After a short distance, and as I was running ahead of schedule. I decided to write down the fare structure for her, I wrote out that Monday to Friday a Senior's fare is only $1 after 7:30pm, and the same $1 on weekends and holidays all day. A Senior's ticket costs $2 and should only be used during rush hour Monday to Friday. Oh, and that a Senior is one who is 65 or older. I handed her the paper, and she smiled. When she was exiting the bus, she grasped my hand within her two hands and mouthed the words 'thank you' with a big, wide smile. As she left, I felt an incredible sense of gratification that I was able to help her. You know, I may have my doubts (that she is not actually a Senior), but I am not about to ask for proof! And should this woman ever come back on to my bus, I will be sure to accept her $1.00 fare - regardless of my doubts.

Chapter 6

Financial Struggles...

IN MY EXPERIENCE, I HAVE NOTICED FOLKS THAT STRUG-gle to provide the proper fare tend to stay at the back of the crowd when boarding a bus or stick tight in the middle of the pack. On this particular night, it was no different as a struggling young couple, a man and woman, were boarding the bus and sticking right in the middle of a group of about 10 people. The man was holding two transfers, one for each of them, but was being careful to cover the bottom of the transfer. The bottom of a transfer indicates the time of expiry. So, covering the bottom of a transfer is often a tell-tale sign of an expired transfer.

The woman looked very uncomfortable. I looked both in the eyes (a technique I use to gauge how uncomfortable people might be), and my gut feeling was that they were using expired transfers. I decided not to ask the man to reveal the full transfer to avoid embarrassing them. Letting them board with my usual 'thank you', the pair continued onto the bus. After about 10 minutes, the woman came up to the front where I keep the garbage container and she put some garbage in it. I looked at her, asking if they were going to be boarding another bus today. She said 'yes', and then with a slight grin, I replied 'well here are two good transfers for both of you to use'. She smiled back and said, 'you could tell, eh?' and I replied, 'yes, you're simply too nice' as she smiled again and continued back to her seat. When she got back, I noticed her telling the man about our exchange. When they got up to exit the bus, I saw the woman deliberately coming to exit via the front door. The man stayed near the rear exit. As the woman made her way to me, she said "thank you so much, you made my day." I replied, "no worries, I know you're good folk". Watching her leave the bus, she met the man, and he looked back at me to mouth the words 'thank you', complete with a smile! Sometimes these feel-good moments arrive when you least expect them, and they really are priceless!

Chapter 7

Too Loud...

HAVE YOU EVER BEEN IN AN ANNOYING SITUATION WHERE the pressure builds up so much that you simply wanted to yell 'SHUT THE F**K UP!' What really annoys me is someone talking extremely loud on the bus with no consideration for others! Well, this night was certainly one of those nights for me. Don't get me wrong, I love a bus where people are relaxed and enjoying themselves... to me it indicates confidence in the driver (from my Coach days – lol).

A couple of young girls, accompanied by their male friend were chatting up a storm. Now, just imagine high pitched, loud voices that rattled every inch of the bus and your spine with continuous nonstop chatter – the guy could not get a word in edge wise. I could not even make out what they were saying, the sounds were piercing my hearing aids and it was becoming a big distraction.

As the trio were departing the bus, I waved the guy over and said to him... very quietly, "Thank you." Puzzled he asked me, "for what?" I replied, "for giving me a break from your friends talking by leaving, I swear they don't breathe when they talk!" He immediately burst out laughing, and the girls (now outside the Bus) asked him what was so funny. He relayed what I told him, and the girls began laughing like hell as I pulled away.

They were good kids, just caught up in each other's company. I think at times, we can lose sight of how loud we can be in confined spaces, especially on a bus with a few people in it. But, sometimes, it really is just too loud.

Chapter 8

"Hey Buddy, Whatcha Doing?" ...

THIS ONE IS AN OLDIE, BUT A GOODIE AND I JUST HAVE TO share it! Late one night, and with only a couple of passengers on the bus, this guy gets on the bus and is clearly feeling no pain and is 'four sheets to the wind - drunk!' Let's just say his back teeth could easily have been floating if they were loose!

As he boarded the bus it's a typical, "sorry buddy I got no money, but I gotta get home." I told him if he behaves and just sits quietly, he can get on. I then asked him where he needed to get off... as I was sure he would be drifting off to sleep soon. He managed to tell me, and off we went.

A few minutes went by, and suddenly he jumps up, panicked, and begins to frantically look behind and even under the seats! I said, "hey buddy, come on up here. What are you looking for?" Without skipping a beat, says "my fu***ng wife!" I replied, "but you boarded the bus alone!" A crazy look came across his face, and with no shame he says, "oh s**t, I left her in the bar!" As I was desperately trying to hold back my laughter I asked, "but why were you looking under the seats?" He then blurts out, "oh s**t, you'd be surprised where I find her!"

Well, I knew he didn't have any money, so I handed him two transfers and told him to go over to that stop across the street and go back, and be sure to get her some safely." As he staggered off the bus he said, "God bless you sir." I began to wonder if he was going to make it, let alone be able to get his wife home. I thought... 'my goodness, a box of popcorn and a can of pop would make this the perfect sitcom!'

On the surface, and with the benefit of storytelling... this sounds funny. But many people are struggling, and it is a wonder we do not hear of these types of stories reflecting personal hardships, and of the struggles to cope. Be kind, because you simply do not know the battles people are dealing with in their lives.

Chapter 9

Happy Birthday...

ANOTHER INTERESTING STORY (FOR ME ANYWAY... LOL). A guy gets on the bus and his Presto card has no funds. I said, "no worries, you can pay by cash." He said that he did not have any change. I said, "no change at all, no problem, because today is your lucky day, and you can pay the Senior fare of $1.00." He reiterated that he had no change at all! "Not even a quarter or a dime, just to put something in?" I asked. "Um no, nothing" was his reply. So, I looked to another guy standing behind 'Mr. No Change,' as he was counting his own change getting ready to deposit it in the fare box.

I then said to the second guy, "today is your lucky day to pay it forward!" He looked back at me confused and I continued, "this guy has no change, so how about you pay the Senior fare $1.00 for him and in turn you can also pay the Senior fare of just $1.00! That way you're only paying $2 instead of the regular $3.75." He was quite pleased and agreed. Happy to move things along I said, "awesome, happy 65th Birthday to the two of you!" Well, 'Mr. No Change' was thoroughly confused by my joke and says to me, "wow - Happy Birthday, buddy!" The 'cherry on top' here is that he then announced that it was my Birthday to the entire bus! He then blurts out, "hey, guess what everyone... it's the bus driver's Birthday today!" And began to sing the 'Happy Birthday' song and then encouraged other passengers to join in the song (many did - lol)! This was hilarious!

You know, it reminded me of my Coach days with the interaction between a Bus driver and passengers! I did not want to ruin the moment... as my Birthday was coming up shortly, so I simply went along with it... lol.

Now, don't be thinking that I am giving out free rides left, right, and center. But we must always use our own discretion when passengers do not have the appropriate fare. As it turns out, it ended up being an early feel-good Birthday gift to myself.

Chapter 10

My New Old Friend...

THIS NEXT STORY WAS A NEW EXPERIENCE FOR ME THAT I just must share. On this particular evening I was picking up passengers at one of our terminals. I noticed an older man crossing the street, about 80 years old. Our eyes met, and he had a look of fear and of helplessness.

I waved for him to come to my bus, and as he did, I asked if everything was alright. He looked back at me very confused and put his palms up as if to say, 'I don't know.' I asked him some more questions, and the only response I could make out was 'Peru.' Realizing he did not speak English, I thought 'oh boy, what to do now?'

I decided to ask my passengers if anyone spoke Spanish and if they would be able to provide some translation assistance. This nice lady and her teenaged son, who were on their way to an appointment at a nearby Hospital, offered to help. Unfortunately, the only information she could get out of this gentleman was that he lived by a river. But there was no river nearby. I soon realized he might be suffering from Dementia or Alzheimer's, and that I just could not leave him alone as he was truly lost and needed help!

I quickly called dispatch to inform them of the situation and to send help. They agreed, and told me to go 'out of service,' and to wait for assistance to arrive. All of the passengers understood... as all of their eyes were fixated on us! Not one passenger complained as they exited the bus, many of which gave me a thumbs up and a smile! Unfortunately, my translator had to leave in order to get to her appointment... so I moved my bus to a vacant spot to await a supervisor.

As we waited for help to arrive, I began thinking of what I could do to connect with this older gentleman. I decided to show him pictures of my grandson and granddaughter to keep him occupied. He simply loved my pictures and videos... as I showed him one of my favorites... my 3-year-old grandson playing his toy drum! He loved it and kept 'cupping and clapping his hands!' What really surprised me was how he was quite taken with how pretty my daughter Danielle was and is!

Finally, help arrived. First a supervisor (Janice Camilleri), then police, then an ambulance. Turns out there was an APB on this man, as his family reported him missing to the Police many hours earlier. Luckily, he matched their description to a 't.'

As the paramedics were about to take him to the hospital... a precaution to have him checked and to be reunited with his family, he forcefully made his way back to me. He then gave me a quick handshake and then a big hug. I held back tears as I thought 'I will never see this man again' but I was obviously happy he would be back with his family, and that all things ended well!

Heading back to my bus, several of the officers (4 of the 5) came over to me, shaking my hand and thanking me profusely. It was obvious they were all very concerned with my new / old friend, and to be honest, it caught me off guard that they would stop to tell me what an incredible job I did, and to take down my email address.

To me, all I had really done was shown a bit of compassion to an old man who appeared lost. Be nice, because you just never know, eh?

Chapter 11

Indian Student on Mother's Day...

THIS STORY INCLUDES A VERY SPECIAL SHOUT-OUT TO MY young Indian friends who are here studying as International Students.

My adventures working out of my particular garage affords me the opportunity to meet all kinds of incredible students from India. These kids are not only full-time students, but many work incredible hours just to pay their incredibly expensive tuition fees. Notwithstanding the cost of their rent, groceries, and utilities. Many of these students are here alone with no family for support, and as such seek solace and support in each other's company! They make incredible connections to last them a lifetime as they are here in very similar circumstances... as their families are also back in India.

This adventure was particularly touching. A young, homesick girl got flowers for her mother to celebrate Mother's Day (she told me she took pictures of the bouquet to at least show her mother). As she boarded my bus, she went all the way to the back of the bus to have a seat. We passed a few stops, and then she started to shyly come back to front of the bus, with a truly special surprise!

She very shyly asked me to accept the flowers she bought for her mother! She continued to say that because I had helped her when she was lost and helped her out on a few occasions when she was short of Bus fare... that her mother would be honoured if she gave the flowers to me!

Me! Just a guy driving a bus. Wow, simply incredible!

Well, this is a 'Happy Mother's Day' to me, too!!!

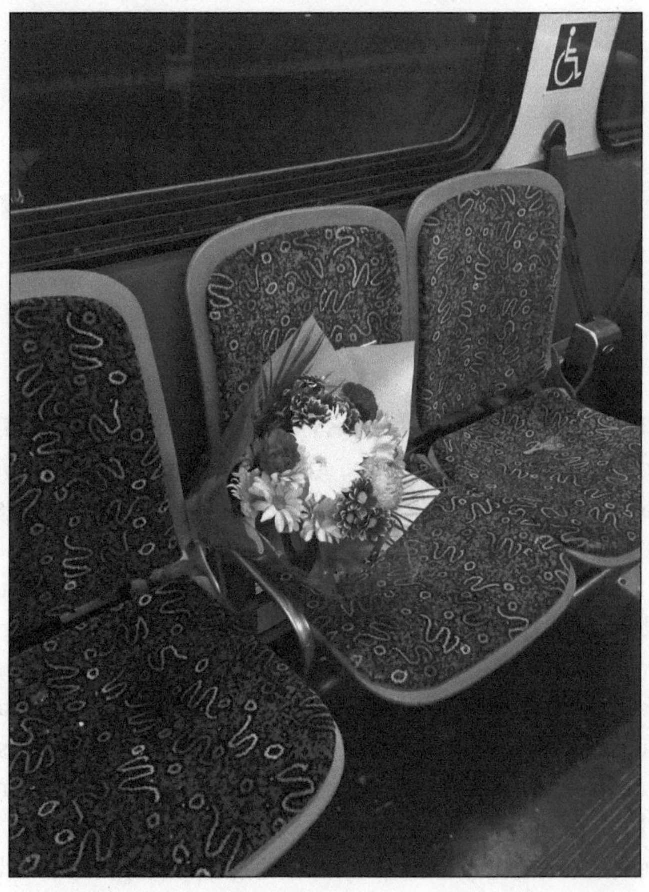

Chapter 12

Belated Mother's Day...

I HAVE NO IDEA WHY... AS I'VE DRIVEN BY THIS LOCATION many, many times, but this wave of emotion ran through me yesterday as I passed it. About four years ago, a young family got on my bus about 9:30 at night. The mother was about 26 years old, with two children: her son, about eight, and her daughter, about six years old.

The bus was nearly empty, and it was a warm dark night with the stars getting ready to light up the skies. In essence... it was truly a beautiful night.

The kids were well behaved and goofing around... as kids with a bond do. It was obvious they loved and cared for each other. But the young mother had this look on her face that has been etched in my memory as I saw it many times with my own mother growing up.

The look is unmistakable to me! For me, it's the look of having the weight of the world on your shoulders. One of hopelessness and despair, a feeling many struggle with daily nowadays I'm afraid.

Well as we were going down the road, I got her attention and motioned for her to come up to me. She looked puzzled, looking around seeing that it was just us and to ensure I was calling her specifically to come up, as she hesitantly obliged.

When she came beside me, I said, “I know it’s none of my business, but are you ok?” She replied “oh, I’m ok thanks.” I then said “well, I vividly remember that look on my mother’s face when we were once evicted from our apartment... one of having the weight of the world on your shoulders!” I decided to continue as she was clinging on my every word, and asked again, “are you sure you’re, ok?”

She began crying and told me of how she had found her boyfriend fooling around on her for the third time, and in fact had just been evicted herself. She continued that she was on her way to her mother’s and that she knew her mother was going to be angry as h**l and would scold her as she always hated her boyfriend.

For this poor young girl, she was in the middle of a storm swirling all around without help in sight, and with no clue as to what to do next! She was no doubt at the lowest level she had ever been in her young life... feeling all alone yet having to take care of her two young children! Her words still sting me to this day, “I just don’t know what to do!”

My heart cried for her, but I could not show her my emotion. She needed empathy and support, not for me to feed into her plight with sympathy. I said, “you are obviously going through a terrible time, but just look at your kids! Look at the love they have for each other and listen to them laughing... you are obviously doing an awesome job as a mother, as well as sheltering them from the grief and stress you are obviously going through.” Hesitant, she replied, “thanks, but I just don’t know.”

I continued, “my mother and family got through it and so will you. Just keep taking it one step at a time and things will work out, believe me I know, and I can see it in you!” Wanting to be reassuring, I continued, “as for your mother, she will act out of her truly unconditional love for you, and she will show her hurt as frustration and anger that her baby is struggling and hurting. This is no doubt tearing her apart inside as she hurts for you, just as it’s tearing you up!”

She looked at me and smiled saying “thanks,” as she went back to her seat. A few stops later as they got up and started to leave, I quickly reached into my pocket and grabbed all the money I had (about $80 I think). Crumpling it up in a ball I handed it to her saying, "please, let me do this and don't count it until you're outside. This will not solve your problems, but just know you are not alone, and your mother is your first step – and there are many support groups out there in many places! Go to a community centre or church and speak with someone... I'm certain they will help! Just continue to do what you're doing and take one step at a time my young friend." She smiled and gave me a big hug as they left my bus.

Well, about 45 minutes later I was coming back and who did I see having dinner in the Popeyes window? But this young family eating and with huge smiles! I continued driving with tears swelling in my eyes comparing her plight with that of my mother's.

I know this is late, but "Happy Belated Mother's Day!" For me, every day is Mother's Day... especially when situations like this remind me of my own mother's strength and unconditional love!

Chapter 13

Kids on the Bus...

A MOTHER WITH HER TWO CHILDREN BOARDED MY BUS, one in a stroller and a girl, aged five or six. This little one had her Mommy's Presto card and tapped for her. I looked down at her smiling and said, "who's a big girl now?" She shyly looked at her mother and they shared huge grins.

They settled in the bus, and we proceeded down the road. Then the little girl began singing 'The wheels on the bus go round and round' song but was a little unsure of the words. No matter, I just loved it and was no doubt driving with my silly grin.

As they were leaving, I began singing it out loud with the correct words. She looked up at me with a grin of pure joy that warmed my heart - what a delight!

Ever since then, every time she sees me and my bus, she gets so excited as they board. God, I love my job! It affords me opportunities to interact with kids which remind me of my own grandchildren.

Chapter 14

Cool Dude, Wanna Free Ride...

ON THIS EVENING AT THE TERMINAL, ALL OF THE PASSENgers had boarded, and I was about to leave... but then, a surprise, of course. This dude gets on my bus. You know the type; a loud - hey look at me type guy who wants to be considered the coolest and toughest dude around (to me a sure sign of insecurity).

Well, he gets on strutting his stuff and he wants a free ride down the street. I said, "do you not have any money?" He replies, "no man, can't you just carry me down so...." While finding his schtick amusing, I began laughing and let him continue to strut his 'tail feathers.' I said "sure, come on let's go." (I've found that making the 'bad asses or very insecure' your friend - makes things so much easier)

As we leave, he then exaggerated his strut on his way to the very back of the bus... he knew everyone was fixated on him. Loving every second of this attention, he gets on his phone and continues to be extremely loud, as if he was deliberately trying to be heard - in a loud crowd, meanwhile no one is talking!

At this point I'm thinking I've got to reel this guy in as this is not "his" bus, and there are about 20 other passengers tolerating his antics. I then yelled back at him, "hey buddy" as I started motioning to him with my right hand to tone it down! As I continued in a loud voice, "let's show a little respect for all the other passengers on the bus, you don't need to be yelling on the phone!"

A bit of a risky move as I knew this might hurt his pride, but frankly I didn't care at this point. I was not about to let him disrespect my passengers - not on my bus!

Well, he shuts up and says back, "hey man, no disrespect intended - I'm sorry you're right!"

We continued to the second stop on the route, and he got off - using the back door saying, "thanks again man, sorry!"

Now, as he walked by the front door, he waves at me while smiling and gives me this signal with his right hand - with what appeared to be an upside down 'O.'

Now, I do not have a clue what it meant, but I would like to think - that he made a new friend and that he felt he could respect. I cut him some slack yet held him accountable, and I felt his response to me was positive. From my viewpoint, he got my respect when he settled down, and even apologized... despite me doing it in front of all the passengers (of which I've noted is a 'no-no' in terms of not embarrassing one's passengers as it can seriously escalate issues).

As I just noted, this is one of my primary rules: to never embarrass a passenger. I always inform or discipline very, very quietly, like when I know they are cheating. Oh, and I lower my reading glasses from the top of my head to the tip of my nose as it really helps me get that serious and mature look...lol

Chapter 15

Old Man and a Bike...

I MET THIS INCREDIBLY NICE OLD MAN TONIGHT, WITH AN amazing laugh and sense of humour. I was at one of the malls we service, and most passengers were on board. I noticed this old man wheeling a bicycle towards me. He was pushing the bike with one hand and had a cane in his other hand. That was a first for me.

He was able to drop the bike-rack into position on the bus but struggled lifting the bike onto it. As I was going to help him, another older man, maybe age 70, also began to help. As I got there, the two of them managed to put the bike on the rack. Solid effort, but it was backwards, so I adjusted it.

Noticing a price tag taped to the bicycle's seat, I said "so did you buy the bike for your grandson?" He replied, "no, it's for me!" I looked at the other man in shock, and the feeling was mutual.

I said, "are you kidding? How old are you?!" He replied, "my birthday is next week, and I'll be 84." I said, "are you serious, you're 84 and still riding???!!!" He says "yep!"

Well, we got back on the bus and proceeded up the road. The number 84 was still rolling around in my head. I said to the old man, "so when was the last time you actually rode a bike?" He replied, "last October, but I fell and broke my hip and haven't ridden since." "And you're getting back in the saddle?" I said jokingly. He started laughing and said "yep, I'm not going to let that stop me!"

I continued, "well perhaps you should get a bunch of bubble wrap and a huge helmet!!! The last thing you need to happen is that you fall again, but this time on the other hip." He starts laughing and says, "think my old hockey equipment would help?"

I said, "come on, seriously, is this bicycle yours and do you intend to ride it?" Again, he replied, "yep!"

When we got to his destination I said, "no worries, I'll help you get the bike off the rack." We both got out to get the bike, and once it was off, I said to him, "please do me a favor, call your son and daughter, anyone, and let them know you got another bike... ok?!" And he says, "you're worried, aren't you?" I said "of course. I realize we all have a crazy kid still inside of us, but even my sense of balance is not what it once was!" And he says, "don't worry, I'll even tell my doctor, I promise" as he shook my hand.

I just hope this old man tells his kids, because as amused as I was at this whole thing, I am truly worried he is going to hurt himself. Age 84 and walking with a cane... he still wants to ride a bicycle! One can only hope he has a guardian angel watching over him, I can't do a lot as a bus driver, but for an 84-year-old man-child riding a bike, there is nothing much I can do.

Chapter 16

A New Family in Town...

TODAY, A YOUNG FAMILY CONSISTING OF A SON AND daughter of about ages 9 and 11 boarded my bus with their mother and father. They were very unsure of our fare structure, and in fact were not sure how to pay.

I told them about the fare for the family, but the father still looked very confused. He just held out money for me to take the appropriate fare. I looked at what he had, which was much less than the actual fare, and simply let them pay with what was in his hand.

I asked if they were new to Canada, or just visiting, and the father noted that they were here to stay from Syria. The father was just so appreciative as I continued saying "well, welcome to Canada!" And then they all looked at me with huge grins.

When they were getting off at their stop, I informed them that the Mall was closing in 10 minutes. With a distinct and strong accent, the father replied, "ok, thank you."

I did not think much of it and continued my route. On my way back, the same young family got on my bus and the father said, "I should have listened more closely to you, the Mall just closed." I wanted to remain positive and reminded him that he can always visit again. I emphasized the good deals this Mall has because it is an actual 'Outlet Mall' where chain stores offer special deals.

We traveled up the road and as they left, they all thanked me. In fact, they kept smiling and waving at me as they walked to their next transfer point. It was not a simple wave, but a heartfelt 'thank you so much' series of waves. What a great experience all around.

Chapter 17

Grumpy Old Man...

'HAPPY SATURDAY.' OR SO I THOUGHT! AN OLD MAN boarded my bus and insisted on a new transfer as his had expired way past the applicable time. Three hours... in essence he wanted a five-hour transfer when transfers are only good for 2 hours. Not to mention when I refused to give him a free transfer, he shortchanged his payment! His entire attitude just rubbed me the wrong way as I have a hard time when folks exhibit an entitled attitude with no sense of responsibility on their end!

I could care less what colour, race, religion, weight, height, sex, disability or looks one is... it simply does not matter to me! If you are not nice to folks, do not expect them to be nice to you, let alone break rules for you.

The sense of entitlement has gone a bit too far in my humble opinion. Yes, we do have rights, but do not expect favors when you disrespect or take advantage of other's good graces.

Sure, he may have been short on money to return home, but he was going into a mall and gave me no explanation. Be honest, tell me the truth and I would bend over backwards to help if I can, but be rude and demanding just gets my 'back up!'

He scowls at me, and I sat firm saying "sorry, no, transfers allow you two hours." Then, he stuck out this huge tongue. I almost started to laugh but managed to keep my laughter in check.

I then said to him, "why should I break the rules for you when you're not being nice?!" He didn't say anything, but simply stuck out his tongue again.

As he left my bus, I actually felt sorry for him as the old saying goes 'once an adult twice a child.' Perhaps he has many issues going on which I am not aware of. I am certain I did not make a new friend today. The scowls continued as he walked down the street while staring at me.

Chapter 18

Old Man and a Bike: An Update...

WELL, GUESS WHO I RAN INTO AGAIN? NOT LITERALLY BUT figuratively (that would be a whole different kind of story to share). Yep, you guessed it... my bike riding old friend of age 84!!!

What a pleasant surprise, as his smile and demeanor was as awesome and pleasant as before, but low and behold he had scratches on his face. I asked him about the scratches, and he shyly said, "that damn bike, I fell into the bushes!" I asked if he was alright. He replied, "oh yes, but that bike is no good!"

I said, "between me and you - there is a time to let go, and perhaps you got off lucky this time... I really think you should give it away or sell it!" He replied, "yea - I think you're right." With a sad look, he continued, "it's just so hard to let go." I then replied, "yea... it's kinda like me and sex." He started laughing. In good form, he replies, "well at least you can get some blue pills!"

Such a nice old man, but as with all of us, sadly there comes a time to let go. As he departs at the end of the line, he comes back to me to say bye, and asks for a transfer because he thinks he's going for a pint. I said, "for you of course... but I need you to promise to get rid of the bike - ok?!" And he says, "yea, I know you're right - I promise!"

I said, "awesome" and I gave him a $5 bill as I continued "your beer is on me my friend, but you have to keep your promise!" He says, "I will, I promise. Thank you, you're a good man," while shaking my hand.

Given the connection I developed with my older friend, I just felt so good!

Don't you know, about 3 weeks later I see this fellow riding up to my bus on a tricycle at the same ole mall and Bus stop. It's my old friend waving at me from his new three-wheeled bicycle with a huge grin on his face! I could not stop laughing, but I tell you one thing; what an incredible old man and I am so pleased to call him my friend!

Chapter 19

Step in Or Stay Silent...

AN OLD MAN DID NOT TAKE WELL TO A JOKE BY A FELLOW passenger. For context, this old man is extremely religious, and with every step is extremely slow and deliberate. In fact, one day it was pouring rain, he had no umbrella, and his pace did not speed up. Never to rush him - I would say, "take your time my old friend!".

Well, he sat directly in front of a much younger guy, 30-ish, wearing a reflective vest, and he appeared to have had a pint or two after work. The younger guy said to the old man, "come on, no need to be so slow - you're still a young buck!"

Well, the old man certainly did not find it funny and gave him a proper tongue lashing. I could only hear parts of it, such as 'you have no idea', 'going to church', 'it's not funny to make fun', etc.,

The younger guy did not reply, but at this point I can only imagine by the look on his face.

I was anticipating having to interject but given the silence in the entire busy bus, I left it alone to play out. The old man got out first, and as he left turns to me and says, "God bless you, my friend!" He has never said that to me in the past. I think he knew I was biting my tongue, as we've had many conversations in the past. I simply said, "to you too my old friend - you take care, eh!" As the young guy leaves my bus, he turns to me and says, "I really didn't mean anything bad to him." I said, "no worries, he's very old but very forgiving, you take care now!"

I am certain their paths may cross again, under very different circumstances. Now, they have much more empathy and understanding for each other.

Chapter 20

Tourette's Syndrome...

THIS PASSENGER HAS BOARDED MY BUS ON MANY OCCAsions, always on the same route, but it set up a really touching moment for me this evening.

Given my limited knowledge of Tourette's Syndrome, I am certain the passenger is afflicted by this condition. Spontaneous uncontrolled physical movements, with spontaneous swearing while yelling out, and sudden mood swings are very typical with him.

Well, I've developed a bit of a bond with him. In fact, tonight, he jumped up with excitement as he saw me driving into the terminal's spot for his route. He was sitting on the curb, and when I honked my horn at him to move, everyone noticed how happy he was to see me. Now bear in mind, this is a man in his 50's, and many sluff him off as being 'touched' and avoid him.

This evening he allowed everyone to board first, and everyone watched when he came on and began exchanging pleasantries with me. First; gently punching me, then smiling endlessly... reaching out to touch my shoulder and offering me a typical Indian blessing with a prayer symbol with his hands.

Well, everyone remained silent and simply watched as he sat alone just behind me. During his entire time on the bus, he was active and loud. Yet, no one was concerned as if they all took their cue from my interaction with him - and my assurance that he is alright and not to be feared.

As he left my bus, he went through his ritual of blessing me and thanking me profusely. I could see all the passengers watching intently. He continued waiving as we drove away.

Then a stop or two later a young couple were getting off and commented "he must have some sort of condition?" I said, "I'm pretty sure it's Tourette's, he's really a very nice guy!" And she says, "you're really good with him, thank you!" Yes, another 'feel good' moment for me!

Chapter 21

New Love...

DO YOU REMEMBER THE DAYS WHEN YOU WERE FIRST IN love and your new spouse walked you to your bus stop and saw you off to work? Even when it was late at night. Hmm... well, neither do I - lol!

Anyway, I have this young couple on my route that do this most nights. In fact, it is so cute that I began waving bye to this young wife as well, and now she waves bye to me too... as we all have a good laugh about it.

Well, last night he forgot his Presto Card. He calls to her asking if she had it, but to no avail! She then starts running back to their basement apartment as we are on a small residential street.

The guy starts to leave the bus, and I said, "hold on, is it far? dang she's fast?!" He said, "no, it's just over there." Knowing the next bus was not for another half an hour - I thought, 'why not wait,' I was a minute early, anyway.

Bam! She is out in a flash and runs back to the bus. I put my hand out the window, and you would have been impressed with the Olympic-style hand off. Laughing, she runs back off the street, to applause from passengers on the bus.

I yelled out, "what a team, just like our Raptors!!!" Resulting in cheers of "Go Raptors Go" on the bus.

Just a great, feel-good moment for all of us on the bus.

Chapter 22

A White Fur Coat...

THIS STORY OCCURRED TWO BLUSTERY COLD WINTERS ago. However, I got a special Birthday request for one of my 'feel-good' stories. Now, this one will be etched in my memory forever... not that it wasn't already - lol.

I was driving in an area that was under construction, and in an industrial area with no sidewalks or bus stops. It was dark out and very poorly lit, not to mention it was literally freezing out with high winds.

I could not help but notice a white fur coat fighting the winds and walking in an area I had not seen anyone walk on this roadway before. This was over train tracks, and on the shoulder of the road.

I instinctively felt something was wrong. I pulled over beside her and opened my door. I asked the lady (35-40) if she was ok. She did not say anything but began crying profusely. I told her to come in and warm up. I reassured her that everything would be ok now and asked where she was going as there was nothing in the area in which she was walking.

Once she calmed down, she noted that she was lost after just being in the area for a job interview and was trying to get home. She said that she had just arrived in Canada a few months ago, and it was daylight when she went for her interview, but now she was lost.

Her English was very broken, and she was still very upset, not to mention still extremely cold. Understanding her was difficult, but I figured out where her home was. I assured her that everything was going to be ok now, and that I could take her to where she could get a bus to go home. This poor girl was walking in the completely wrong direction with absolutely no bus going in the direction she was walking.

She began crying again and hugged me. My God, she was bringing me to tears given all her struggles. And you know, not a passenger said a peep in a very crowded bus of folks trying to get home after a miserably cold snowy day as they just watched intently.

Well, I got her to the Transfers point for her to get to where she needed. We arrived, and many people were also exiting at this junction. Not only did I get another big hug, but many of the other passengers commended me for stopping to help this lady. My passengers seemed really pleased to witness such a good deed and in fact to be a part of helping her as no one complained. When your gut tells you something is wrong, listen... I have found that it is generally right.

Chapter 23

She Felt I Was Mean and Heartless...

A YOUNG LADY GOT ON MY BUS WITH HER SHOES IN ONE hand and was in the process of eating a banana with the other. "I'm sorry, but you need to finish the banana and have your shoes on while in the bus as we are not permitted to eat or walk barefooted in the bus."

She looked at me angrily and told me that she had just bought a new pair of shoes for her new job and that her feet were bleeding and killing her. It was impossible for her to walk in these new shoes. I then said, "I'm really sorry but the shoes need to be on your your feet," as she began to put the banana peel in the garbage container. She grudgingly obliged and went and sat down.

As she left, she came by and gave me an earful about my being insensitive and that she had checked on the internet and read that non messy snacks are permitted. I simply replied with "well, it's obviously my judgement call and I view bananas as being messy, as discarded skins pose a hazard for my passengers, and I've had to pick up many discarded peels left behind by previous riders."

She did not continue the conversation and left, very clearly agitated. As she walked, well, limped, due to the new shoes, to reach her connecting bus, I noticed her blood-stained bandage at the back of her heel. I felt sorry for her, as her emotions were no doubt all over the place with a new job and her new shoes perhaps ruining her day.

Well, yesterday she got on my bus again at the same stop by the bank tower. This time wearing flats. She came in shyly and said, "I'm really sorry about yesterday. I was rude and very disrespectful to you." I said, "no you weren't, you were frustrated and just trying to put things together from your own perspective and I understood and felt for you - believe it or not." She was engaged, so I continued, "the safety of all my passengers is number one, I know the banana peel is a minor one, but your banana was almost finished, and the garbage can was right here." As it was important for her to understand, I continued, "as for your bleeding foot, I could not take the chance of blood in the bus as I would have to take the bus out of service due to other passengers coming into contact with any form of body fluid."

She smiled, said "thank you" and went to sit down. This time, as she left, she came back to me and said, "I'm really still very sorry!" I then said, "look, don't worry about it, hell, I would have carried you if I could - that's how bad I felt...you just needed a bit of time to think about things." She then had this look of someone dying to hug someone. She quickly put her arms around me and said," thank you so much, I'm still so sorry!" At which point I gave her a gentle 'it's ok' squeeze.

Her smile lit up my bus and she said, "have a great weekend my new friend!"

Yep, it made my night!

Chapter 24

A Whirlwind of a Day...

A LOCAL UNIVERSITY IN OUR CITY HAS A PROGRAM THAT deploys a two-part card system to board a bus and confirm proof of payment. One card has name/information, and the other card has the picture/photo ID. Both must be shown in unison to board and ride the bus.

Well, a couple of stops into my first trip of the day a young male student got on my bus and showed me only the information portion of his card. There was no picture portion. I said to him "sorry buddy, but I need to see the picture portion as well." He got very upset and said, "why are you harassing me, don't you trust me? You can see I have it!" I then said "true, I can see it, but I can't see your picture." He then took it out of his wallet and shoved it in my face about 8 to 10 inches away! I immediately backed up and said, "what are you doing, you know that's not necessary?!" He then puts it back in his wallet and he starts to rant about how I am disrespecting him, when no other driver ever asks him to see his picture.

I pulled the bus over and said to him, "look, this really is not necessary, you can either go have a seat or get off and wait for the next bus." He then physically gets up in my space to intimidate me. I immediately said, "back off buddy are you threatening me? Do you see that camera filming you?!" He backed up and looked up at the camera, and as he did that I said, "you are causing your own problems now make up your mind!"

Just as I said that a male passenger in the back of the Bus yells out "hey a**hole, leave the driver and let him do his job!" The kid looks at him and sees him now standing and says, "well he's harassing me." The passenger then says, "who are you b*ll-sh*tting, we could hear the whole thing - now shut the f**k up and let him do his job!" The student then leaves me and goes back and the two of them continue talking as he goes and sits down.

A few stops later, the passenger, who stood up for me, was leaving and came by the front door. We did not say much, but I said, "thanks for the support, buddy," and he replied with "what a jerk!"

Well, a couple of stops later, the student comes up to the front and I thought, 'ok, here we go.' To my amazement he says, "hey man, I'm sorry for the way I acted." Surprised, I said "listen it's over, but if I can give you any advice, that attitude will cause you problems, you seem like a good kid, don't let that attitude ruin things for you."

At which point he says, "I know... can I get off here?" I said "sure, you take care eh" as we fist bumped.

Later that day, the passenger who stood up for me boarded my bus on my return trip. When he got on, he says "hey buddy, good to see you again, boy that kid was a punk!" I said "yea, but he must be a new University student feeling new pressures as he obviously is unsure of the expectations of using his student pass." The guy says "yea I suppose, but he sure was a jerk! I couldn't do your job!" As he laughs and he goes back to sit down. When he left, I merely said, "thanks buddy."

He replied with, "for you, anytime!" Yep, a "feel good" moment for me!

Later, on my way back up, this extremely pretty mother, maybe in her late 30's, with her young daughter, maybe 11 or 12, boarded my bus. The mother looked very confused and showed me a piece of paper with all kinds of scribbling on it. She simply points to a hotel name they were heading for, and I said, "no problem - it's just about 10 stops up... stay near the front so I can see you and I'll let you know when we're there."

As we approached the hotel, I waved to her to come up. When she did, I asked her "so where are you from?" She replied in a very strong accent "Jordan." I said, "wow, welcome to Canada, how long have you been here?" She replied, "about 12 years." I said, "what?" She starts laughing and says, "oh no, we're not tourists, we're going for an audition for my daughter for a movie." I said, "that's awesome I'm sure your daughter will do well!" She says, "well we'll see." Her daughter was looking up at me and I said to her "you're going to do awesome, just be yourself and I know you will do well!"

They both smiled as they left and even gave me two thumbs up as they crossed the street in front of my bus. Well, about 4 hours later I saw them on the street trying to figure out how to get back. I honked my horn to call them over and then they came running. They got on the bus and were so appreciative as they were totally lost. I said, "so how did it go?" The mother then replied, "we learned it was all just a scam, and even all the other parents there were saying the same thing. Very unprofessional and they simply only wanted people's money." I said, "oh dear that's too bad - well, better to find out now rather than later, because when it comes to your daughter - better safe than sorry!"

They both stayed behind me and were trying to figure something out on the phone. I said, "what are you looking for?" It turned out they were trying to figure out the mother's Uber App. I asked about their next destination. The daughter replies with "to the subway." I said, "ok no worries, I will drop you off where you can take one bus and it will get you right to the Subway, and then you can get an Uber from there if you wish." They both replied, "thank you!" They stayed by my side and as they left, both were so appreciative of my support and help that they both gave me a hug. My God, what a lovely surprise.

Well, just after the mother and daughter left my bus, ahead were First Responders; Ambulance, Police, and our own Enforcement, at one of our parked buses with a supervisor beside it. I pulled over just past the commotion and the Supervisor began directing the passengers from that bus on to mine. As the Supervisor continued marshalling people over, he says, "you folks are in luck - you've got one of our finest drivers!" You know, it made me feel great to hear that I was appreciated. Then again, the Supervisor could have just been easing passenger tension after what must have been an emotional ordeal for them. Regardless, it was great to hear!

We continued down the road when a blind man with his dog and guitar got on the bus. I made sure he was on his desired bus route and asked where they were getting off. Such a beautiful Labrador Retriever, but the dog lies down right in the middle of the aisle. I hesitated to say anything until I had to. Sure enough, a few stops later more folks came on and I had to say something. The blind man was so apologetic and said, "I'm so sorry, come on Lady come beside me." He was as gentle with her as she was with him. Such a beautiful bond between them.

Well, now I'm on my final round trip, and just a couple of stops into the trip one of my regulars gets on, as she is on her way to work for the night shift (normally, she gets on alone and then two of her coworkers join her much later as their warehouse is near the end of my trip). They all get off just prior at a Tim Hortons due to my bus being the last bus... and their shift does not start for another hour and a half. As such they relax, kill time, and have a coffee before walking the rest of the way for the start of their shift.

As she boarded my bus I said, "we missed you last week... were you ok?" And she replies, "so you didn't hear?" I said, "hear what?" She says, "I found my 32-year-old son in his bedroom after hanging himself." I said, "Oh my God, no... is he ok?" And she started bawling and said "no, he died." I was left utterly speechless and just let her cry on my shoulder. I then said, "I'm so sorry, God I wish I could find words to ease your pain!" She mumbles, "its ok, well I'm not really, but what can I do?" She went to sit down as she continued to cry. As I began driving, I said, "is there anyone I can call for you?" And she says, "no, that's more than kind though." I was driving with tears in my eyes as I could not bear to look at her, even though I kept glancing over in her direction.

We got about halfway up when one of her coworkers got on and joined her. What a terrific guy. He was upbeat with her and even got her laughing, so obviously they had a good working relationship. All the way up so many thoughts ran through my head as suicide is in and of itself such a complex issue to rationalize...it is simply impossible. From a simple point of view, suicide is merely a transference of pain and never a solution. As the pair left my bus at the Tim Horton's, she came to me and simply gave me a hug. No words exchanged between us.

This, my family, and friends, was not a typical day. My God, I was exhausted at the end of it all. Be safe eh and let us never take anything for granted.

Chapter 25

Thanksgiving...

GOING TO WORK ON THANKSGIVING MAY SEEM ODD TO some, but because I'm grateful most days, it really is not all that bad. Besides, we have a special dinner planned for this in a few nights.

Well, as it goes, my very first passenger had issues and I had not even sat down in my driver's seat yet!

I was relieving another driver and was waiting for the bus in one of our terminals. Well, this scruffy looking middle-aged man was coming alongside the curb on a bicycle. He was cycling while holding a two-wheeled dolly packed with items up to the handles, all tied up.

The guy stopped right where the bus needed to stop. As such, I informed him that I was going to take over the bus and could he move up a bit more so the bus could park at its designated spot. The guy starts with a very negative attitude and says he personally can stop anywhere he wants because he has special status, and we must accommodate him. I asked what status he was referring to and he pulled out his CNIB pass which allows him not to pay a fare while boarding.

I said, "that's fine," but asked if he could still move up a bit more. He continued with his negative attitude complaining that he is continuously harassed because he rides a bike with a legal designation of being blind, and because of his dolly packed to the gills.

I replied that I'm not questioning the degree of his blindness, nor of his dolly or its contents, just a simple 'move up so the bus can stop properly.'

He moves up and the bus I am taking over pulls up. The guy then realizes that my bus is not the one he wants and gets angry and more frustrated. He hauls his bike and dolly off to the side while cussing. As I began driving, I thought, 'let's hope my day gets better!'

It sure did! Waiting for me at one of the stops is a regular East Indian fellow with his wife and their 5 or 6-year-old daughter. The little girl always gets excited when she sees me. Well, she's eating a hamburger as she gets in, and even though eating food is not permitted, I turned a blind eye and simply said to her "my goodness that's a big hamburger! Who is a big girl now?!" Shyly, she gave me a huge smile and walked back to a seat with her parents following her.

As we are traveling down the road, the father comes up to me and says "you know, my daughter talks about you and gets so excited when she sees you coming down the road! I know this is not much, but please have a coffee or hot chocolate on us and happy Thanksgiving. You really are special." He hands me his completed McDonalds card for a free drink. All I could think of to say was "my friend, to have such a special little girl, you guys are doing something right. You truly are blessed. Thank you!"

A few stops later my little friend comes up and puts her wrapper in the garbage and says, "happy thanksgiving!" I smiled at her and said, "to you as well my little friend, happy Thanksgiving!"

Well, later in the day a tall and slender older Sikh gentleman boarded my bus, on his regular trip to work. Usually, he never talks but has a very respectful and distinguished air about him.

As he got up to leave, I gave him my usual "have a great shift my friend." This time, he surprises me as he starts talking. He says, "I don't have much, but have this." He handed me a small Hazelnut Almond Coffee Creamer.

Shocked, I said, "are you sure?" He replied "yes, I have a few at home and brought this just for you. Happy Thanksgiving!"

I tell you; it blew me away... never in my wildest thoughts had I ever imagined someone giving me a Coffee Creamer as a gift and feeling so humbled and grateful. It was a symbolic gift from his heart at Thanksgiving.

I was almost in tears as I thanked him and said, "Happy Thanksgiving my friend!" He exited the Bus and simply stood in the doorway facing me with his hands in a prayer position. I did the same and said "thanks again... have a great shift my friend" as I closed the doors and drove off.

Later in my shift a young Nigerian girl gets on my bus with a bag in hand. I recognized her as another regular on Sundays, as she makes her way home from work. She did not say anything, but I greeted her with my typical "hello my young friend" as she boarded my bus.

As she leaves, she comes to the front and extends the bag to me. I asked her "did someone leave it behind?" And she replied "no, I brought this for you, Happy Thanksgiving." I said, "for me, why?" She said, "because you always make me feel welcome in your Bus, and for that I'm thankful - so Happy Thanksgiving!"

My God, I did my best not to tear up and said, "you truly are special, thank you so much!!!" She simply turned and walked away. When I had the chance later in my shift, I opened the bag to see what she had given me. It was an orange chocolate fudge cake. How sweet!

Later in my shift an older Chinese gentleman gets on my bus. He just finished his shift at a Dim Sum Restaurant and is on his way home. We normally exchange minor pleasantries, but never talk beyond that. But this time, as he leaves, he turns in the doorway he put his hand on his heart and says "Happy Thanksgiving" ... in a very broken Chinese accent. I replied, "Happy Thanksgiving to you as well my friend!" But you know, his hand gesture on his heart made it just so much more special and sincere.

As I continued driving a young Muslim fellow boarded my bus. I have seen him with his wife a few times, and as she wears a Burka, I felt he was Muslim. He hands me a bag and says "I cooked this in the restaurant tonight and brought you some dinner. It's not much, but it's my gift to you on your Thanksgiving."

I said, “oh my friend, it’s not only my Thanksgiving - it’s our Thanksgiving! It’s a time when we can all give thanks for what we have.” He said “true, so thank you!” He went to sit down.

I felt disappointed later, as he left via the back doors, which did not give me the opportunity to thank him again. He made something just for me, very special. Of course, once I had the chance, I opened the bag and container to see what it was. Low and behold it was a vegetarian chow-mein.

Now I am nearing the end of my shift and I spot my classy Jamaican old friend running for my bus, halfway between stops! He is not hard to spot; he always has a white hat, the same style my father used to wear, paired with his usual stylish suit. He has a way about him that puts a smile on everyone’s face. As he gets on my bus, he says “ya save me again... me, I’m always late, thank you!” When he was leaving my bus, he came to the front and said “ya know, God blesses good people like you. Happy Thanksgiving.”

You know, it is times like these that no matter what our cultural difference may be, we all have a reason to be thankful!

Chapter 26

Stolen Transfers...

I WAS AT ONE OF OUR TERMINALS AND HAD TO USE THE facilities. A lot of drivers are very reluctant to allow passengers on our buses unattended due to security reasons, as drivers have had their personal possessions stolen.

Well, I am not one of them and allowed a young fellow in and closed the doors. Even though the doors were closed, he would still be able to get out of the back doors if needed.

After my break (to relieve myself... lol), I was walking back to the bus and saw this fellow with long hair inside of my bus, right at the front. I knew he was not the passenger I had let on. Continuing to approach, I realized it definitely was not the passenger I had let in.

I opened the doors and asked him what he was doing and how he got in! He nonchalantly says, "I pulled the doors open and got in." I then told him that this bus is equipped with cameras, and that no one is allowed in until a driver lets them in! He then said it was not the correct route, and that he made a mistake. I quickly replied, "ok then, bye, don't do that again."

As he left, I got in my bus, and asked the passenger I had let in prior to leaving for the washroom "how did he get in the bus?" The passenger replied, "he pulled the doors open and then went to your seat." He then continued "I told him he should wait outside, but he just ignored me. He then started reaching for your transfers when you startled him. I'm sure he took some transfers!"

I then did something we are specifically trained not to do! I quickly went to where the guy had gone, on another platform at the Terminal. I approached him saying, "did you steal some transfers? First you break into my bus, and now you compound your problems by stealing transfers?!" Startled he says, "look I'm sorry, you stopped me before I got any!"

Now I'm angry and he could see it! I said, "look, don't you ever do that again. Everything you did was caught on camera. If you need help or are short of funds, I will help you out but steal and you are only creating problems for yourself that you obviously don't need."

I continued, "so you honestly didn't steal any transfers?" He said, "honestly, no." I said, "ok, I won't call our Enforcement or Police, but don't ever do that again! If you need help, just be honest with me and tell me." He then humbly says, "I promise, I won't - honest!"

I then left him, but as I was walking back to my bus, a supervisor was coincidently bringing another driver to retrieve another driver whose bus had broken down. I stopped him and leaned into his window telling him what had just happened. The Supervisor asked, "do you want me to deal with him?" and I said "no, I think I got through to him and doubt he'll do it again. Besides, by looking at him I think he's already struggling with problems long before this."

I got back onto my bus and saw the passenger walking away. I truly felt sorry for the guy. Hopefully, there is no next time. But if he had come to me, I would have helped him out as we all struggle at times.

Chapter 27

Job Interview...

A YOUNG GIRL MISSED HER BUS STOP UP BY A RACETRACK and now had to travel way out of her way.

She approached me and wanted to get off. I asked her where she was going as she looked very confused. She told me, and I said "well, don't get off here, no bus will get you back to where you want to go, but this one."

I told her to stay on my bus until we got to the Subway... as she would just be waiting out in the cold for the next bus on the route – which would be me anyway. When we got to the Subway, I explained to her where to go to get back on my bus, as the Subway is the termination point where everyone has to exit.

As I was in our waiting area at the Subway, I saw her going the wrong way! I got off my bus and yelled at her to get her attention. Well, everyone on the street is looking at me as some crazed driver, but I did not care as long as I got her attention. She came running across the street to me, so I could finally stop yelling... lol. I then told her again where our stop was for her to get back on as she was still very confused (at times looking for a tree in a forest can be difficult).

Well, it turned out she was new to Canada, and was going for a job interview at a restaurant very close to the Racetrack. Assuming she was going to be late for her interview, I asked her what time her interview was scheduled for. Turns out I could get her back to where she needed to be with half an hour to spare, as she had given herself ample time to get to her destination.

As we were traveling, I gave her some interview tips and told her to see herself in the position and to be confident. At first, she was very insecure as it would be her first job in Canada if she got it. I said "look, have faith in yourself, you have already proven yourself in this type of work. Believe in yourself... and, your interviewer will see it, and will see you in the position."

She said, "thank you so much, you were just what I needed" as she went and sat down. Once we got to her stop, I called out to her, and she got up and came to me. I said, "now you go and be confident... just be yourself and see yourself in that position." She did not say anything in response but nodded and smiled giving me a fist bump.

Well, a couple of hours later I was doing a completely different route. And who gets on my bus? The same young girl! At first, she thought she was on the wrong bus, but I assured her that she was on the correct route to reach home.

I asked her how her interview went, and she said she needed to go back the next day for a second interview with the owner. The Manager really felt that she would be a good fit for their restaurant. I said, "good for you, I knew you would do well just by the fact you had prepared for any delays in not being late for your interview in the first place."

Well, her stop came up as she had to transfer onto another city's Bus. She came up to me and said, "you know, I think I was really lucky to meet you. You helped me incredibly today, thank you so much" as she gave me a big hug.

Yep, another feel good moment on my Bus!

Chapter 28

A Humbling Experience...

THIS ONE BLEW ME AWAY AND IS TRULY HUMBLING.

We have just begun a new sign-up period at work. As such, I am doing a route I have never done before during the week but have done it on weekends. Because of this, I am meeting all kinds of new passengers.

We were traveling along when this young fellow comes up to me from his seat and asks me if I normally do a particular route, because he recognized my voice. I said, "I have done that route many times, but we do many routes."

He continued, "well, my girlfriend talks about you all the time as one of her favorite drivers! In fact, we've met a couple of times as well on that route!" I then said, "sorry, I'm still at a loss." He then says her name, but I still am unsure as to who she is.

Then, he describes her and where she lives and gets off. It began to click in, and I asked him if she's seen pictures of my grandson, and he begins laughing and says "yes, she loves him, and I can't begin to tell you how much she really enjoys riding your bus because of the way you treat all of your passengers." He continued, "she says, it's truly remarkable how welcomed you make all your passengers feel! And it's so true because I was watching you today!"

Feeling humbled and a bit embarrassed I said, "well I'm very fortunate because I sincerely love my job. Just think, I get to play with a big toy, drive - which I love doing, and I get to meet a lot of awesome people like you; who out of the blue has come up to me to compliment me as a friend. That in and of itself is worth an extra transfer!!!"

He then continued "well, she's going to be blown away that I met you way up here and be jealous as hell!" Laughing, I replied, "well I'll no doubt be doing that route in the new year, so I'll get to see you guys again soon."

His tone quickly changed to one of disappointment when he said, "well not really, because I'm heading back home to Australia." I then said, "you know, I do remember you now - but never heard you speak. My God I love an Aussie accent! Well, you'll be back soon, no?" He then said something like, "Yea, but just not sure when. I'm just go glad I got to see you again before I left, and my girlfriend is going to go nuts and be jealous as hell!"

All I could do was give him a bit of an embarrassed laugh because he was making me feel like some sort of celebrity. Then, I suppose all good things come to an end, because his stop was coming up. This was his transfer spot, back to the route in which we met each other. We shook hands and he said, "it truly was a pleasure chatting with you, you truly are an awesome driver - thank you!"

Now, many times I feel blessed and yesterday was certainly one of those days. Just think, be nice to a stranger and you will be rewarded ten-fold.

Yep, another feel-good moment on my bus!

Chapter 29

Bus Etiquette 101...

AS YOU MIGHT RECALL, I AM WORKING ON A NEW WEEKDAY route with all kinds of new passengers. I think many passengers are taken aback by my style. At first, I may appear to them as their grumpy old grandfather. However, they soon realize that my actions merely reflect my attitude of accountability and that I care for each one of my passengers sincerely.

Some feel I have a magnetic personality. But do not crowd me or block the entrance/exit just to be at the very front. Even if you want to see where we are going, or to be the first one off at a particular stop. In dealing with this, when we arrive at a bus stop with 3 or more folks waiting to board, I always say, "for all folks exiting the bus, please use the back doors to exit. Once again please use the back doors to exit the bus, thank you."

I find the procedure effectively educates riders by reinforcing that staying at the front renders them last off the bus. Not just that, but the procedure is much more efficient as there is a flow of movement as passengers embark and disembark at the same time. As soon as people realize this, you can tell they appreciate this procedure. It really benefits all parties involved.

Along the same lines, I hate leaving anyone behind because of a packed bus. I will pack my passengers like Sardines in a can (if need be), especially in inclement weather. Saying things like "folks, please move right to the back and up the stairs as I refuse to leave anyone behind when we have lots of room in the back of the bus. Don't worry, when we are at your stop, I will wait for you to get off, thank you." If I don't see anyone moving or just a few I will continue with the same speech, as many times as it takes to get folks moving.

I have even tried to lighten the mood by saying, "I realize we're packed like sardines in a can with a stranger right beside you... but tell ya what, turn to that stranger right now and smile. Bam! You just made a new friend!" Invariably, they always comply and some even smile!

Then of course there's the mother with a baby in a stroller at the back of the crowd waiting to board the bus. Folks tend to be aggressive when boarding to get the best seat. Well, I keep the doors closed. I get out of my seat and raise a bench, asking passengers to kindly relocate to accommodate the baby if the seat or bench is occupied. Once I raise the bench, I get back in my seat, with people clearly seeing what I just did. The odd person tried to drop the bench, but I kept an eye on it and told them to not adjust the bench or seat, as it is for a baby about to board the bus.

You know, I even had an older gentleman come up to me and say, "I must say, you run a good bus." He caught me off guard, but it took me back to when I was oh so much younger and was complimented by a respected supervisor. It made me feel great!

Chapter 30

Thanks Laddie...

AS I NOTED PREVIOUSLY, I HAVE BEEN INTRODUCING A whole new set of passengers to my expectations of bus etiquette and procedures. Really important things like not crowding the front and exiting via the back doors.

Well, guess what? Even on Black Friday my passengers were orderly despite the bus being packed to the gills. Today, it ran very smoothly as passengers boarded and exited my bus in perfect sync. Sure, I made my announcements of "please exit the bus via the back doors," but they already knew what to do and were prepared.

Not only that, but at two different stops a mother with a stroller was about to board the bus. A couple of regular passengers were already raising the seats to accommodate the stroller, even before mom and the baby boarded. Amazing! Each time I made sure to compliment the Good Samaritans, with smiles of acknowledgment from many passengers.

Well, wouldn't you know it, a young girl and her dog Laddie were about to board the bus and I thought 'oh boy I hope the passengers are ok with the dog as the bus was already packed.'

Laddie was on my bus the previous day and had a hard time as she cried in fear. Well, I asked the young girl to stay up front with me so I could try to control the environment or mood in the bus.

She obliged and in a loud voice I asked her (again, I already knew of Laddie's accident with a car and his subsequent fear), about his car accident and of why she was scared. I did that so the passengers could hear and perhaps develop some compassion and empathy for Laddie. Then, I stared patting Laddie and folks began oohing and awing as Laddie cuddled up to me. Folks could see his fear disappearing a bit as I comforted her. Laddie still cried, but at least passengers were empathetic to her fears. It was like the entire bus was pulling for her to be at ease as I was keeping an eye on them through my rear-view mirror. Then, at one point she raised her paw for me to hold it, and again I could hear sighs of joy from passengers who kept watching.

The young girl was so appreciative as she knew exactly what I was doing, and when she left with Laddie she said, "I can't thank you enough, thank you!" Her smile melted my heart.

We were getting near the end of the run and a gentleman came up to me and said, "you know, just yesterday I phoned in a compliment about you, but not knowing your name I simply gave them the bus number, route number and time. What is your name?" Well, when I told him he continued "well, I'm calling them back as day after day you impress me with your caring nature and of how you make your passengers at ease by running an efficient and caring bus. Especially when the scared dog came on!"

What can I say folks? I love dogs and today Laddie brought out the best in me.

Chapter 31

Peaches and Cream - Not...

I CAN IMAGINE THAT FOLKS READING MY ADVENTURES might think everything is all 'sunshine and roses' on my bus. Well, think again! Just yesterday, I reported to work only to find out we had 3 drivers physically assaulted by the same passenger as he went from route to route to perpetrate his attacks.

As drivers we walk a fine line from; fare collection, personal conduct on the bus, ensuring the safety of our passengers from each other, the safe operation of the actual bus itself, maintaining a time schedule, and adjusting to traffic and weather conditions. Not to mention customer service for all, as some folks think only of themselves.

Sure, I do all I can to control not only the physical environment of my bus, but of one's social or personal experience on my bus by being respectful and compassionate. But, as you all know, regardless of your efforts, it's impossible to please everyone. Sure, I love my job, but my whole motivation behind these stories was because of my distaste for all the negativity we are bombarded with day in, day out.

Just be kind to each other as we are all caregivers for our own environment and as such, each other.

Chapter 32

After All These Years...

THIS PAST SUNDAY BEGAN LIKE MOST DAYS, BUT BY THE time my shift was over I thought, 'what an awesome shift!'

One of my first passengers of the day was a fellow I met about six years ago on my bus and he reminded me of the bearded guy from the musical group 'Walk Off the Earth.' Unfortunately, this man from the musical group died a few years ago - R.I.P. Mike Taylor. Well, this passenger normally just goes and sits down, but today for some reason he stood by me and began chatting.

We were traveling down a four-lane highway, two lanes each way, when we came upon an accident. It had just occurred, as there were no flashing flights, first responders, etc. We were totally blocked with nowhere to go. So, I called to inform our Control Centre, who then notified Emergency Services.

As we sat there, my bearded friend and I discovered we had much in common. Such as where we grew up in Toronto, the areas of Toronto we are familiar with, places we have worked, and even similar roles in the workplace. Albeit, about 15 years apart. In fact, he went to the same school where my daughter is currently a teacher. Small world!

After we had been delayed quite some time, the Ambulance, the Fire Department, Police, and our supervisor all left the scene as the Highway was cleared for us to continue. But now my bearded passenger was not just a passenger, but a good friend.

Obviously, I am way behind schedule and our dispatch had arranged for coverage of the trips/route I was missing. Once I was back on route, and they plugged me in once I got back to a location, so I could continue my route as scheduled.

Low and behold, one my first passengers back on route was drunker-than-a-skunk, but I have seen him before and he does not usually pose a problem for passengers, other than a foul odor. Shockingly (not quite) he has no fare. So, I asked him if he was going to a certain location on the route and he nodded and said, "yes." I then said, "ok no problem, just remember sit nice and be good!"

Turns out he is not going to where I thought he might be going. Somewhere to warm up and get a hot meal. Nope, but he continued right to the end, even as I went back to him to try and talk to him. Well, as we are nearing the end of the trip my bus begins stalling and quits running!

I called our Control Centre to notify them of the problem and informed them I would need a change off bus (replacement Bus) once I arrived at the terminal. I knew I could make it as I merely had to wait a minute or so and would be able to restart the bus after each time it stalled.

Sure enough, as I stopped in the terminal to let the passengers off, the bus stopped running again! But now, the drunk fellow does not want to get off the bus as required. A young female driver was now taking over my bus, as I was going to take over another Bus... is now in the bus with me.

I called Control informing them of the situation of our stubborn passenger, and they gave us guidance to simply open all the doors and to exit the Bus as they were sending a Supervisor and our Enforcement. We did, and after a minute or two he quietly left. I then left and proceeded to my new Bus.

I ended up leaving a few minutes late from the terminal... much to the chagrin of irritated passengers. They all made sure to let me know, even though I told them why I was a bit late. At least I had a functioning bus! As we proceeded, I thought I should call Control to cancel the Supervisor who was on his/her way along with enforcement as the drunk passenger had left the bus on his own. As I was talking to them, I said, "let's hope I don't have to call you again!"

About ten minutes later, coins begin jamming up in my fare-box. And I simply could not clear the change or get them to drop into the farebox. As such, I had to call in and report the problem. They then instructed me to put the fare-box on bypass, which then renders the counter out of order and the coins simply drop into the box. I have never done this, as it is normally a supervisor's responsibility, and I was not sure how to do it. Turns out one needs to remove as many coins as possible from the top of the box, and then put it on bypass; something I did not know.

We continued and all is fine... for now.

Then, on my final trip of the night, this nice old man gets on my bus and hands me a baggy of mixed nuts that he put together for me. As he hands it to me, he says, "this is just a little something for you in case I don't see you before your Christmas." I then said, "oh my goodness, thank you, but you didn't have to do that!" I then said, "hey wait a minute, did these have chocolate on them before?!" He just started laughing and laughing and said, "oh no, I save those for other drivers!"

Yep, another awesome day on my bus!

Chapter 33

Respect and Compassion...

I HAD THIS YOUNG FELLOW BOARD MY BUS THIS PAST Sunday at about 7pm. He did not have any fare. The bus was almost empty, it was dark out, and I was about ten stops from the end of the route.

He begins to beg, and I mean beg for a ride. I looked at him and said, "please, don't ever beg on my bus... as no one rides for free as there is a price for everything in life. I don't care what you put in if you can... as long as you're trying." He then says, "hey man, can you simply give me a ride?"

His cavalier attitude really rubbed me the wrong way as my message was not getting through to him. I said, "you look like a good kid - why are you disrespecting not only yourself, but your mother? Look, growing up my family was very poor, and I had two jobs when I was 16. One job gave me spending money, and the other was to help my mom. How would your mother feel if she knew you were begging for rides?"

It blew him away, almost as if he was in shock as he stood there speechless. So, I continued, "Look it's obvious you're a good kid... just don't disrespect yourself or your mother. If you're short of funds, no worries.

All bus drivers will cut you slack if they don't feel you're taking them or the system for granted."

As I continued, I paused and said, "I'm sorry, I don't mean to lecture you, but begging gets easier and easier to do as you get used to it. Please, don't fall into that trap. Never lose respect for you or your mother." Again, I paused and said "here's a transfer, go ahead and have a seat, I'm sorry I came down on you so hard. I say these things because I honestly care!" Still in shock he says, "thanks man" and goes to sit down.

As he got off the bus, he came up to me and says, "thanks man, you really give new meaning to respect, thank you!" As he gives me a fist bump.

You know, I'm certain I get away with this behaviour because when I lower my glasses on my nose I look like a grizzled sincere old man!

Later that night on my final trip to the terminal, I was very close to the same stop! It was cold, dark, and about 10:30pm. This young girl gets on the bus. She looks visibly upset and says, "I'm so sorry, but I lost my Presto card." I looked at her and said, don't worry I found a transfer for you."

She is almost in tears and says, "oh my God, thank you so much!" Dang, she almost had me in tears with her sincerity, as she was visibly upset.

When we got to the terminal and at the conclusion of an 8-and-a-half-hour shift, she comes up to me and says, "you are so nice, thank you again!" I said, "no worries, just call in to Presto and tell them you lost your card so they can freeze it, and when you get your new card, they will transfer your balance as long as you had it registered!"

Suddenly, she really starts bawling. This is an emotional, hard cry. I said, "are you ok?" And she replies, "I've just had a terrible day and I really don't understand why."

I said, "look, you don't need to rationalize it, the bottom line is it's real because you feel it. Just recognizing that you don't understand the 'whys' is a good sign in itself - am I making any sense?!" She says, "well I guess so."

I could tell she was still upset, and said, "are you waiting for another bus now?" And she says "yes, it should be here in 14 minutes." It was dark and cold as hell, not to mention not one of our safer terminals, especially late at night! So, I said to her, "look, which way are you going now as I'm going back to the garage, and you will be going down a dark street... can give you a ride? I really don't feel good leaving you here when you're so visibly upset!" She replies, "yes, that's the way I need to go." I said, "ok, no worries just stay on."

As we left, she stayed near me. I just kept talking to her about the ups and downs of life. About the good times and bad times being no different than a pendulum on a clock which goes back and forth, from one side being good times and then on the other side are our bad times. I said, "always know that no matter how bad your bad times are - good times are guaranteed to follow. You just must believe and keep moving!"

I then said, can I show you something that I guarantee will make you smile?" She says, "sure." So, I pulled over and stopped my bus. I took out my cell phone and began playing a video for her of my son and grandson (3 years old) goofing around to some music just before my grandson's bath. I continued driving while she watched the video, and it took her to another place emotionally as she began grinning from ear to ear. Believe me, it's an awesome video which reminds me of what an awesome son I have.

Anyway, she hands me back the phone and says, "what an awesome video, your grandson is so adorable!" I said, "yea, I'm truly blessed!!!" She then says, "oh I'm so sorry, but I need to get off at the lights." I then said, "no problem, are you sure you're, ok?" And she says, "yes, I can't thank you enough!" And gives me a fist bump!!! You know, I still don't know why she was so upset, but I am glad that when we parted, she seemed better.

As I continued my drive to the garage, I simply thought; well, it's been a long day, but definitely a good day!

Chapter 34

Mixed Emotions...

WELL, ONE RECENT EVENING WAS THE LAST WEEKNIGHT for this route and schedule as we were heading into our Christmas schedule for the next two weeks. It has been seven weeks, and not only have I learned the nuances and patterns of passengers on this route, but they have learned of my expectations, and at times wacky sense of humour. I like to keep people on their toes.

It was freezing a few weeks ago and there were many new Canadians who rode my bus during this period. It afforded me the opportunity to help 'care-for' and teach many how to dress for freezing temperatures.

Remember, many of our passengers have never experienced such cold temperatures and have no idea how to dress. Not to mention the lack of money to buy suitable clothing and footwear. I truly feel sad when I see a young guy wearing flip-flops in the snow with no socks! The kid must be freezing, but simply does not have someone to tell him "Hey, put some socks and boots on, it's cold and you could get sick!" (Not that one need be told, but habits can be hard to break!)

I had a few such kids on my bus, and this fellow who was about 30 years old boarded my bus, and he has Down Syndrome. He was dressed properly so I thought I was going to use him as an example for these kids as we have spoken before, and I have a good rapport with him.

I welcomed him on the bus, and as usual and I said, "Hi buddy, it's been a while how are you? I see you're dressed for the cold." He replied with "oh yea, have to stay warm and dry." I continued, "I've got my long-johns under my pants and even a couple of loose shirts under this sweater - you?!" He says, "for sure I do, this is too cold! "You going let me off at my street?" I said, "of course buddy, don't I always do that?" We shared a laugh. Well, his street comes, and he bids me farewell. All along I could tell we were being watched and folks were listening. These new immigrant kids are bright and are eager to learn. As such, I know they will do great and will make awesome Canadians!

You know, an example of this is a small group of about six kids I met about six weeks ago. Our first encounter was at night, and they were all huddled in a shelter. As I drove up, no one came out to make me aware that they wanted the bus. Sensing they may want my bus; I stopped and honked my horn. At this point, they all came running out!

As they boarded, I said, "you know several different buses service this stop, so it's your responsibility to come out to make the driver aware and know you want their bus." Their reply was, "oh we're sorry." I then continued, "well, if you don't - you may just end up simply watching the bus drive by without stopping." The next few days, they were all coming out swiftly as the bus approached.

Well, one night it was freezing, and I felt bad as I was going in the opposite direction and nearing the end of the route. I could see just how cold they were. When I turned around at the end and began the trip back to where they were. When they boarded, I told them to hold on as I wanted to talk to them as a group.

As they stood there, I told them that rather than staying at their stop waiting for me when it was freezing, to cross the street and to get on my bus as I am heading in the opposite direction. At least then they would be inside the bus where it is warm. Then, when we got to the terminal they would need to get off, but they should simply go to the other side and wait for me to begin my trip back. All the while being warm and inside a sheltered place. They tried it the next night and it worked out tremendously!

They have been doing it ever since I told them, and I know they appreciated my caring for them with their actions this particular night. You see, I told them this was my last week on their route and that they would have a new driver next week.

Well, on my last night they blew me away as when each of them got on my Bus - each one had a Candy Cane in hand for me! As they handed it to me, each one wished me a Merry Christmas and added a personal sentiment such as 'we are going to miss you, thank you, you are awesome!' It just made me feel so special. As they left my bus for the final time, each one came up to the front to wish me a final goodbye and to thank me for caring for them.

Another priceless moment for me!

Chapter 35

Christmas Day...

YEP, I WORKED CHRISTMAS DAY... I WILL EXPLAIN THAT one later....

You know, many folks experience such a wide range of emotions on joyous days of celebration. From extreme frustration and loneliness to the joy of belonging to a 'family,' be they by blood or of heart.

Just yesterday, prior to my shift, I was doing a bit of shopping and a mother was very angry at her 10-year-old for wanting a box of cookies. The child was not pestering or obnoxious about it, just simply asking his mother if she could buy his favorite box of cookies. Obviously, the mother was frustrated over other issues bothering her and her son accidentally pushed her buttons! She lashed out and scolded him as he apparently should have known they could not afford them, after she had already gone over her Christmas shopping budget.

I thought, what a sad state some are in as she was lashing out at her own child, she no doubt loves more than anything. She was hurting incredibly with financial issues and in fact was adding to her own pain before she could calm down in order to put things into perspective.

Earlier on my bus, one of my first passengers was a fellow with muscle control issues who could not speak. He got on rudely and does not even pay a fare...simply giving me a backhanded wave with his hand - his palm down and raises his hand while breaking his wrist - in that he does not have to pay. Well, he continues and rudely kicks a passenger sitting in the priority seating section out of their seat - even though there were another 6 seats available for him to use in the 'priority sitting area.'

That was it, I got out of my seat and went back to address him. I stood in front of him and said, "you come on this bus, not offering to pay the required fare and then you have the nerve to kick that nice young fellow out of his seat when you have 6 other priority sitting seats to sit in? What gives you that right?!" (Definitely not condoned by my company and my trainers would go nuts on me for leaving my seat to address this individual!)

Well, he sort of squeals back at me but does the Italian hand signal on his chin for "get lost!" I then said, "don't you swear at me, this is Christmas, and this is how you behave?!" His tone immediately changes and offers a peace offering by wanting to shake my hand in an apologetic manner. I said "ok, but if you want respect, show respect," and went back to my seat. I thought to myself, I hope he's just having a bad day, and that he is not always that bitter - regardless of his special needs.

Immediately following that, a very nice Indian fellow wearing a Turban got on with his family and every single one in his family wished me a very Merry Christmas. I just sat there in awe as they uplifted my spirits and put a smile back on my face and heart.

By far, this Christmas Day - most of my passengers were East Indian as most Christians were no doubt celebrating Christmas with their families. But you know, it blew me away the number of non-Christians who went out of their way to wish me a Merry Christmas! I would say at least 75%. Smiling and obviously sincere in their wishes.

It was such a great feeling all day long, and I must admit it left me humbled. I began thinking of how some Christians treat other cultural communities or for that matter other Religions during their festive times such as Diwali or Hanukah.

I have noted before how prior to Christmas, I put in my destination sign 'Happy Holidays' (there was no option to put Happy Hanukkah or Happy Diwali) simply to be inclusive (we didn't have that option at the time but do now). For those of other religions and cultures and even for those who do not believe, I simply want to spread good cheer for all, not just Christians! Then, on Christmas Day I change my sign to read Merry Christmas.

Here we go again... another Caucasian fellow with issues gets on my bus and wants to go to the Airport. I told him "I don't go there, but I can take you to the terminal where you can get a Bus that does." He simply goes and sits down. I then said to him, "hey buddy do you have a fare or transfer?" He says, "I showed you, here." He pulls up his sleeve to show me his hospital wrist band (even though it's not a legitimate fare equivalent, I tend to pardon them and let them on). I then said, "well, your hospital wrist band is not a transfer, but no worries." I then handed him an actual transfer so he could continue on his way when he departed my bus as a good will gesture.

Well, he went and sat in the priority section in the front of the bus. As we are traveling along, he stretches out his legs so far that they are now blocking the aisle. We got to a stop and about 3 guys got on the bus and had to maneuver around this guy's outstretched legs. I then blurted out "hey buddy, can you pull your legs in, why should people have to maneuver around you? That is just plain inconsiderate." Startled, he just glared at me, so I glared right back at him. After about a 5 second stare-down, I turned to begin driving and to ease the tension. He then pulled his legs in and says, "sorry man." As he leaves my bus, he comes up to me and says, "I'm really sorry man, have a good Christmas." I said, "you too buddy Merry Christmas!"

Well, my shift is nearing its end and I'm tired as I am battling a cold bug while reflecting on my Christmas shift. I thought, the most Christmas love I felt today was from our non-Christian community. The main thing that stood out to me on this day was the incredible outpouring of love and good wishes from our Indian community that made my day and of Christmas.

You know, to me Christmas is about the giving of our love. But far too many get wrapped up in the expectations and fanfare of a commercialized Christmas. In all honesty I decided to work this Christmas to ease the stress on my kids. I wanted them and their growing families to begin their family traditions for my grandchildren to be in their homes. It's times like these that we put so much pressure on ourselves by trying to squeeze everyone in by visiting and sharing Christmas with those close to us.

Well, as a single father, I simply told them that our Christmas can be later in the week, with everyone coming over. To me it is not about a particular day, but about caring and loving each other every day. Just knowing I helped ease the stress of trying to squeeze everyone in at Christmas, and I still get an amazing day with my kids and grandchildren to continue our Christmas celebration, is simply awesome in my eyes and heart. From my family to yours, Merry Christmas/Happy Holidays!!

Chapter 36

Special Needs...

I FINISHED MY FIRST TRIP AND WAS HEADING OUT OF ONE of our articulating 60-foot buses... the longer snake type, for a bathroom break. As I was going out the back door, I noticed a passenger still on the bus. Perhaps he missed his stop, so I offered some help. I asked him, "hi buddy, did you miss your stop?" He replied with a simple, "no." I then said, "no? Then where are you going?" At which he replied "north." Right away I knew something was not quite right, so I continued "well, we just came south and I'm just trying to help you out if you need it, where did you get on?" He replied with the location about 15 minutes north of the terminal. I said, "so you got on the wrong bus as you wanted to go north, right?" He said, "no, why are you bothering me? Am I not allowed to stay on?" I then said, "of course you can stay on, and I'm not bothering you, I'm just trying to help if you are unsure where you are going. Where do you want to get off?" Very agitated he replied "look, I'm just going way north, but you keep bothering me!" That was my cue to back off as he was dealing with his own issues, and I had to de-escalate the situation.

So, I replied, "no worries, buddy, I'm only trying to help if you need it, I'm just heading to use the bathroom, I'll be back in a minute." I thought to myself that perhaps he was too embarrassed to admit he just wanted to stay out of the cold with nowhere to go, or he was dealing with his own issues. I rushed back from the washroom because I did not want to leave him on the bus alone for too long. Once I got back to the bus, we began our trek north.

Some 45 minutes later the fellow gets up and comes up to the front. I was not sure what he wanted or what his intent was, so I quickly asked him "hey buddy, do you need a new Transfer for your next bus?" And he replied with "no, I pay by Presto, but I have a question, why do you talk so loud?" Startled, I replied, "ya, I know I can tend to do that, you see I wear Hearing Aids and with all the background noise I lose sight as to how loud I can get" as I showed him my two Hearing Aids. Shocked, he replied "oh, sorry" and he simply left the bus.

I am still not certain what his issue was, but my gut told me he simply wanted out of the cold but was too embarrassed to admit it. Ironic, because if he had simply told me this, I would have let him ride my bus for as long as I was working.

Later that night a mother with a baby in stroller boarded my bus. As she got on, I asked her how far she was going to determine if she should raise a bench in the front to accommodate the stroller. She noted that she was going almost all the way to the end, a 45-minute ride, so I raised the bench, and she was appreciative. As I began driving, I noticed she was standing beside the stroller. I then thought, there is no need for her to stand so long with so many empty seats available. I asked her why she was standing as it's such a long ride to her stop, and she replied "well, I can't, the seat is taken." Immediately I thought this was not right so I pulled the bus over to see why she could not sit. As I went back, there was a lady simply sitting in the seat that the mother would need to hold her stroller and just looked up confused.

I asked the lady verbally and by using hand gestures to move to any number of seats in the immediate area so the mother could sit. Immediately, she got up and moved, still looking confused. I then said, "thank you so much," and the Chinese word for thank you. I was perplexed and confused as to why it was not obvious to the lady sitting, but simply thought, perhaps she has special needs and was not aware of what was going on. All I know is, she was very polite and smiled, especially when I said thank you in Chinese.

We continued down the road with very few people on the bus, and I began hearing noises from a phone or tablet. I then said, "sorry, but whoever has their phone on speaker please take it off and use your earbuds." The mother with the baby spoke up and said, "oh sorry, it's my son's Tablet as I use it to amuse him as he is Autistic, I'll turn it down." I said "awesome, thank you but no worries as he has special needs." As we continued down the road, we began a conversation which of course included my grandchildren. Shortly after another young couple got on with their baby in a stroller.

You know, as parents we are all confronted with the question 'does my child have any special needs I should be aware of and how would I know?' Well, when I was a parent, I also thought about this and how to identify Autism in our own children. I then thought, why not ask the mother with the child who has Autism? I am certain the parents who were sitting across may also be interested as to what triggered her having her son assessed. So, I asked "I hope you don't mind me asking as it has crossed my mind with my own grandchildren, but what was it that triggered you to have your son assessed - especially for Autism?" She immediately said, "of course I don't mind. He wasn't responding to his name or other verbal cues, so I had a feeling something was wrong." I said, "good for you, far too often we can sluff things off thinking my child is just fine!" I continued, "you know, at least now you've given your son a head start in support for his special needs with agencies available these days. If you ignored this, he would no doubt miss out on tools available to address his needs, good for you!"

This immediately struck a nerve with the young family sitting across and they began talking up a storm... my instincts were right! Shortly after the young family got off and it was just me and the original mother and son... we continued our discussion. I then said, "you know this has been an interesting shift in terms of folks with special needs." She said, "how is that?" I said, "well, essentially, we all have special needs... they simply differ with each one of us! Me, I have hearing aids, others may have various forms of Mental issues, and others may have Physical issues.

Essentially, at least when we recognize and address our issues, we are better off.

I continued, "even in this ride with you, three passengers got on the bus and left that have special needs! Did you notice the fellow with the blue jacket? Well, if I'm too nice or soft with him he reacts very negatively, but when I am firm, he keeps his anger issues in check as I do it with respect and treat him as my buddy." She said, I did notice that he really liked you, but I never thought of anything being wrong with him." I then said, "well, special needs are not always visible." No different than that lady with the green coat. I know she has bad knees, so I always kneel the bus without her asking, and she appreciates it. Then there was that young fellow with the blue jacket with a hoody. Although he did not have a white cane, he is legally blind and that is why I ensured I knew where he wanted to get off, so would not miss his stop." She then replied, "I must admit I thought it was odd that you asked him." I then continued, "the bottom line is, we all have needs, yet we're all ok... there is no real 'normal' as it is comparable to others, and we're not all the same. Regardless of your son's needs, your love is unconditional. In fact, because of his special needs, you no doubt love him even more. You are truly blessed!"

With that she gave me a huge grin and smiled saying "thank you so much, you made my day" as she left my bus.

Yep, my job has its awesome moments, and that was certainly one!

Chapter 37

A New Immigrant...

A PARTICULAR SUNDAY BEGAN MUCH AS USUAL WITH nothing extraordinary happening. That was until a young girl came running for the bus. I was on schedule, and besides, if someone makes an extra effort by running to catch my bus I will wait. Unless of course they are across the street, and it is illegal or dangerous for them to cross the street or if I am running late as our requirement is to pick up folks at the stop. Now, most times folks are very appreciative, but this young girl said nothing and simply walked by.

I noticed that after about ten minutes she came and stood by the front and stayed there for the balance of her trip. Then, as she was getting off, she gently taps me on the shoulder and says, "I'm so sorry for not thanking you for waiting for me! But I've not had a good time as I'm new to Canada and it's been hard. I can't get over how nice you are to passengers, the way you greet them and thank everyone. I just had to come up and watch you!"

It certainly caught me off guard. I replied, "I'm sorry to hear you're struggling - where are you from?" And, she replied, "Afghanistan." I said, "oh dear, so many problems there. Even though you're struggling, are you glad you came to Canada?" And she said, "oh yes, but it's people like you who are making it easier for me, thank you!" I simply smiled saying, "no, thank you... you just made my day!"

Chapter 38

Valentine's Day...

A YOUNG FAMILY ENTERED MY BUS AND STAYED IN THE front section as they had a stroller. They had two boys, one about 3 years old and the other about 8 months old. The family instantly reminded me of my son's family, and of my grandsons.

As they settled in, they instantly connected with an old man sitting directly across from them with his walker. They began conversing in Polish or a similar sounding language, so all was good.

The youngest son, not to be outdone, began to scream. Not unlike my youngest grandson when he wants something and is relentless. It is piercing and designed to get your immediate attention, and the object of what they want!

When my grandson does it, I simply manhandle him in a playful way and start eating him on his ribs as he begins a real belly laugh. Well, this father has not yet mastered my technique, but then they are on a bus and this little guy is bundled tight in his snow suit.

Anyway, the father brings the young toddler just behind me to distract him from whatever might have been unsettling the child. For some reason watching me drive kind of soothes the child. I then told the father how similar his two sons were to my son's sons!

I continued and said, "you know, this son is going to have lots of money when he grows up!" The father looks at me as though I'm crazy! I said, "you watch, he obviously is determined to get what he wants and is adamant about it! It must drive you crazy, eh?" He replied, "oh yes, it's frustrating as he won't give up!" I then said, "yea, but when he looks at you with those eyes and smiles - your heart doubles in size I bet!" With wide eyes he says, "you are so right."

I said, "you know, at his age he can't tell you what's bothering him or of what he wants... the screeching is just him talking to you and it's up to you to learn his language without getting bent out of shape, eh!" He smiles and says, "you are so right, and I'm already having difficulty to learn English!"

I then said, "my young friend, you truly are blessed, trust me!" He replied with "I know, we tried so hard and now we have two beautiful boys!" At that moment the mother came up with the other son in hand and their stroller as they were getting off at the next stop.

The mother then says to me, "you know, I was listening to the two of you and I just loved it! I hope you have a wonderful Valentine's Day and May God Bless you and your family – you are very special!"

You know that short ride and exchange with that young family was all I needed to fuel my heart this Valentine's Day...for this single fella! lol

Chapter 39

Family Day...

SOMETIMES, WELL MANY TIMES, PASSENGERS BLOW ME away with their acts of kindness.

I know that negative behaviour is noticed immediately and seems to really resonate with us as we are inundated with it in the media. For some people, this can be an everyday occurrence in their life. And, as the saying goes, 'if you look for bad, you will find it.'

No different than someone walking or rushing for a bus they are about to miss and give up on angrily. They do this without even a wave to let the driver know they want the bus, and simply keep walking.

I tell people time and time again, let it be the driver's decision to either stop or wait for you. If you do not let the Bus driver know you want the Bus... the decision will always be no. That is not to say a driver can or will always stop or wait. Perhaps, we simply do not know or are unaware, or are 10 minutes behind and the passengers already on the bus are anxious to make their connections. Drivers cannot assume without folks communicating with us what the passengers' intentions are.

I have used the analogy of someone in a pub or at an event and there is a person they want to meet. If they do not ask or say something, how is that special person to know - for them to say yes? As such, the answer will always be no! Give that special someone a chance to say yes, and do not always assume the worst.

Anyway, yesterday several subtle good deeds stood out to me by a variety of passengers. The first was someone just getting off my bus informing me that an old man was coming up the street for the bus, and for me to wait. Had he not let me know, I would no doubt have driven on as I was in a busy area and focused on my driving.

Another was a young kid in the bus who noticed a mother with a baby in a stroller waiting to board the bus. He simply got off the bench he was on, raised it for her, and walked to the back of the bus without any need for recognition.

Later in the day an older man with a walker was boarding and was immediately offered help getting on the bus by a guy who was just getting off. Simple acts of kindness by strangers, for strangers.

Then there were the two girls getting on the bus with bags of takeout food in containers. As they were boarding, I jokingly put both hands out as if they were delivering it for me. Startled, she looks up and starts laughing. I said, pointing to my belly, "it may appear full, but it's empty" as I began laughing. Suddenly, she says, "sure you can try some, you just may like it!" I quickly replied, "oh no, I'm just joking, but thank you so much!" She continued, "are you sure? You are more than welcomed to try some!" I said, "I'm sure, you are too kind" as they proceeded to the back of the bus.

Later as they were getting off, they walked by the back doors to exit via the front. As they were getting off, she begins taking out the top container and wants me to take it. Now I am feeling guilty for having enticed her generosity. I quickly said, "oh no, you are far too kind and seriously I was only joking, my belly is full", as I laughed.

She then startled me and said, "you're always so kind to us, you are more than welcome to this." Humbled and a bit embarrassed I said, "tell you what, how about you bring me the same treat next Sunday at the same time but in a much smaller container." She looked at me and said, "I think I can do that because we're working the same shift next week." I said, "you are just so nice, you just made my day, thank you!"

Acts of kindness surround us - we simply need to notice them. In the end, are we not all family on this crazy planet?!

Chapter 40

COVID-19...

WITH ALL THE HYPE AND HYSTERIA SURROUNDING THE COVID 19 Virus, I figured it would be an interesting shift on an upcoming Sunday.

Well, on my first of 9 trips a beautiful old friend got on my bus and stayed right up beside me with her walker, only travelling three stops. She said to me, "I hope you don't mind, but I'm only going to do a bit of shopping before it gets too crazy!" I said, "for you my friend, of course not!" I then continued, "you know, I really wish they would allow only Seniors to shop for the first 2 hours so that you don't have to deal with the hassle and panic buyers!" She replied with, "oh dear, I wouldn't want to inconvenience anyone." She continued, "you know, I don't fear for myself... I've lived a long life... I fear for the young who have so much to live for ahead of them!" Her compassion for others made me appreciate my old dear friend that much more.

On another trip, another dear old friend had just finished her shopping and was heading home. Disgruntled she said to me, "for the life of me I can't find any Hand Sanitizer!" She continued, "I promised my neighbor who has a newborn beautiful baby that I would check the store for her as she is very worried and can't find any!" I then said to her, "well hold on" as I pulled over and stopped my bus. I went into my backpack and gave her a bottle which I keep in reserve. I said to her, "here is a spare bottle I have, and you are free to do with it whatever you want. Keep it for yourself, or feel free to give it to your friend!" My God, her eyes began tearing up and she said, "you truly are special. Are you sure?" I said, "for you, of course, I'm sure. I have more at home and if you need another one just meet me again next week at the same time and I'll be sure to have another bottle for you!" As I was getting back into my seat, she quickly gave me a hug and said, "God bless you!"

Later, a middle-aged man got on my bus and began berating the shoppers he had just finished doing battle within a large grocery store with bare shelves. His frustration was so obvious that I simply felt it best to listen and to wait for a question to deescalate his anger and frustration. After what seemed like eternity, he asked me, "have you gone shopping recently?" I said, "oh yes, and it was nuts!!! But you know what I saw. It was people who are being bombarded with warnings and panic by the media, that the hoarding or panic buying is merely a means for people trying to get a sense of having a bit of control in their lives. In a way, a way to comfort themselves in a sense of being prepared or at least doing what they can to cope in these crazy times." He looked at me as though I was off my rocker and says..." damn, you may have a point there, but it's all so crazy!" I said I know, "just keep a wet rag by your toilette should you run out of toilette paper or cut your paper towels in half!" He began laughing as he got off the bus and says, "good one buddy, have a great day!"

A little later, as I was heading south, a young kid got on my bus with a Long-Board Roller Board. I said to him, "you know my young friend, even when I was your age, I'd kill myself on one of those!" He smiled and simply went to the back of the bus. After a few stops he got out and began racing me!

Obviously, I was not going to race him, but simply drove according to our schedule, but my God this kid was good, even going uphill. Halfway down the route he caught up to me and boarded the bus again. I said to him, "boy, you are good my young friend! But do not be so good that you do not fear a nasty fall. After all, going that fast one slip and you could wipe someone out. Not to mention wiping out yourself. This kid was not even wearing a helmet. He said, "yea that is true, no problem, I'll be safe!" He later got off the bus and came by the front to give me a wave goodbye.

Funny, but on my second last trip he gets on my bus and simply goes to give me a fist bump. Instead, I offer my elbow, and quickly he laughs and does the same as he goes and sits down at the back of the bus.

Now it's dark, and an older rider who is quite the character is between stops. I know where he is going, and he is quite a way away to the next stop. With buses half-an-hour apart on Sundays, I stopped and opened my doors. He begins laughing and says, "you going my way?!" I started laughing and said "ya, but just don't tell my boss eh!"

We got up to where passengers connect to another transit system and most folks begin exiting the bus. My young friend with the skateboard comes by and says, "you know, now you really got my respect by picking up that old man! Next Sunday, you and me, your bus against my skateboard!" We both laughed, and I said, "anytime, but you be inside my bus with your skateboard!"

You know, I thought that was it as I began my final trip of the day/evening. I got about halfway down and a young mother and her son of about 12 got on and were going shopping. I said to her, "are you sure the store is open or that anything is left on the shelves?!" She replied with, "well, with 3 children home for 3 weeks, I just finished work and hopefully they still have some fruits and vegetables." Concerned, I said, "well no matter what they have, it'll have to do eh?!" She said, "so true, regardless - it will have to do." I continued, "you know that's a great attitude, don't worry about what you have no control over. Simply get what you can, and tonight the stores will stock up again for tomorrow." I then said, "how are you going to get back, you realize there are no buses going north eh...?!" She said, "oh yes, we will just get Uber or call a Taxi." I said, "why not have your husband come and pick you guys up?" And she began laughing and said, "oh no, we don't have a car, he failed his driving test four times, and I failed it six times!" I said, "well what can I say? be safe and keep laughing in these crazy times!"

Next up in this longer entry: an episode of the old woman from Midland who is the youngest of 27 children! I asked her if there were any twins or triplets in the family and she said no! Throughout the ride she kept rambling on about her favorite driver on another route, and about how he always “razzes” her with jokes! I said to her, “well, just tell him that you forgot a bag of nuts you are saving for him, as you still have some with the chocolate on them!” I tell you; she couldn’t stop laughing!!! And said, “I’ve got to remember that one... that will fix him!”

Yes, I had a great day. Be safe out there, and don’t panic. Wash your hands and practice social distancing. Not necessarily for yourself, but for my mother who is 93, and others who may be at risk.

Chapter 41

COVID-19: A Sunday update...

WHAT AN INTERESTING DAY. OUR TRANSIT SYSTEM WAS encouraging Social and Physical distancing for drivers and passengers alike. As such, was allowing for free rides and isolating our drivers by partitioning our area from passengers. To accomplish this, they were allowing for only rear door boarding and offloading.

Obviously, if a passenger required the bus to be knelt, we would allow them to board and disembark from the front where we can kneel the bus. Many showed remarkable courtesy and cooperation. Many were very confused as this was clearly out of the norm. I had one fellow come up to me after he boarded with a 5-dollar bill, and asked me "where can I put this?" I said, "well, you can simply give it to me, just ignore the sign saying your ride is free!" He looked at the sign and began laughing as he put the money into his pocket! Some folks slinked into the bus as though they were doing something wrong. I must admit, it was kind of funny at times as passengers are just not used to entering via the back doors and then not paying at all, in our system... anyway.

One event that really got me was a young student who was studying to become a Chemistry Professor at a University when he is done. He is a foreign student working two part time jobs while studying full time. He rides my bus every Sunday and is extremely polite. When I first met him, I just thought he was a young scrawny, nerdy kid. But as the weeks came and went, I grew to really admire his determination and willpower to become the Professor he is working on becoming.

My young friend always has his huge thick Chemistry book and if we are not chatting, he sits and studies. Well, because the area he boards the bus is not well lit, I told him to activate his phone and simply wave it, so it makes him visible at the stop for drivers to see him.

As I pulled over to pick him up, I noticed he was shivering as it was cold and all he was wearing was a T-shirt. As soon as he got on, I asked him, "are you crazy, where is your coat? You are going to get sick; did you forget it somewhere?" He replied, "well I gave it away." I said, "you did what?" He continued, "well, on my way to work today I met this homeless guy, and he asked me for money for a coffee, of which I didn't have!" I then said, "and what does that have to do with you not having a coat?" He replied, "I could see he was so cold, and not wanting him to get sick, I offered him my coat instead." I said, "you did what?! Did you not think of what you were going to do or wear on your way home?" He then says, "oh yes, I knew I'd be freezing, but I have another coat at home, and he didn't." Immediately I said to him, "you know that is awesome - what you did! You know what, your ride is free tonight!" He begins a hearty laugh and raises the sign that notes rides were free!

You know, his compassion simply blew me away. My skinny, scrawny young kid is gaining my respect and admiration every week. We are in troubled times, yet there is so much good still out there. Stay safe my friends, and keep an eye for those in need, eh.

Chapter 42

Another COVID-19 Episode...

I TOOK PART OF MY VACATION TO SELF-ISOLATE AND WAS just reflecting on my last shift driving my bus, while at home. We were only allowing for rear door boarding and disembarking, accessibility requirements aside. Most people walked in just fine, but some were very disorientated as it was not normal, and as I noted previously, it was humorous at times as folks dealt with their confusion.

Well, I could not help observing a well-dressed young lady with a small travel suitcase in tow, simply standing by the doors within the passageway in the middle of the bus. Note: I tend to wait until I need to ask someone to move, as my assumptions can backfire as their replies can be, "I'm about to get off - is this not allowed?!" Oops.

Anyway, a few stops go by with no requirement to stop as no one wanted to board or leave. Then we approached a stop where some young people wanted to get on. As they boarded, the young lady turned sideways to allow them on, but I felt I had to speak up and address her not distancing herself for the sake of others. I said out loud so she could hear, "excuse me mam, but in light of social distancing can you please move away from the rear doors so that folks don't have to squeeze by you?"

Note: I try to never single someone out whereby embarrassing them and getting a snarky response as they attempt to save face. Well, she responded, "I'm getting off at the next stop" in an angry voice. I simply responded, "that may be so, but you've been there for 6 stops now. How are we to know when you are getting off?" I deliberately used the plural "we" to ensure other passengers felt ownership of the situation for all of us on the bus. The young lady's retort was, "well, I work in the Airline industry and know full well what's going on!" Just as I was about to reply another lady spoke up, "then you should know better, shut up and move for the sake of others!" Wham-bam, thank-you-ma'am! The young good-looking lady with her traveling suitcase and feeling a sense of entitlement, had just been scolded and humbly took her seat. I felt embarrassed for her, but tough love can be painful at times, right?

Please folks, for your sake and for the sake of others, let's think of others and not just ourselves.

Chapter 43

Not My Bus, But COVID-19 Related...

I HAVE PLACED MYSELF IN SELF-ISOLATION FOR TWO weeks. Not because of any symptoms, but because I was in very close contact with someone who tested positive. As such, it has been encouraging to see the actions my company has been taking. You know, we can all point out improvements to actions taken by our employers, but at least the actions taken are finally proactive and in the right direction.

Anyway, in preparing for my return to the driver's seat I needed more masks and gloves as our company is not providing them yet, but at least is now allowing us to wear them.

Well, yesterday I purchased 4 four packages of face masks (20 for $10) from my small IDA Drug store. My first stop was to my sons to have a bit of a reunion with my grandsons. Albeit sadly, at 20 feet apart. At least I was able to drop off his package of masks. But, while at my son's house, his in-laws were there too. Everyone was on the front lawn, keeping a safe distance. Turns out they needed masks too, so I gave them a package of mine as I knew I could stop off at my little drug store on the way home.

When I got to my drug store, I noticed the price was now 20 for $20. They had doubled the price! I questioned him about it, and he put the blame on his wholesaler. I then said to him, "that may well be true, but it's obvious you are purchasing them in bulk and repackaging them. Now four hours later you've doubled the price!?"

I then said, "regardless of whose fault it is, the reputation and perception of being a price gouger will not serve you well, and you may very well be reported to the phone number for folks to report such price gouging. You may have to justify this as a result." He sharply replies with, "honestly, it's not my fault!" With my patience being tested, I replied "perhaps, but it certainly does not look like it." Regardless of his reason, he sells me a package for the original price. I returned today, and the price is back up to 20 masks for $10. These are trying times, but do not let them change you! Be safe, my friends.

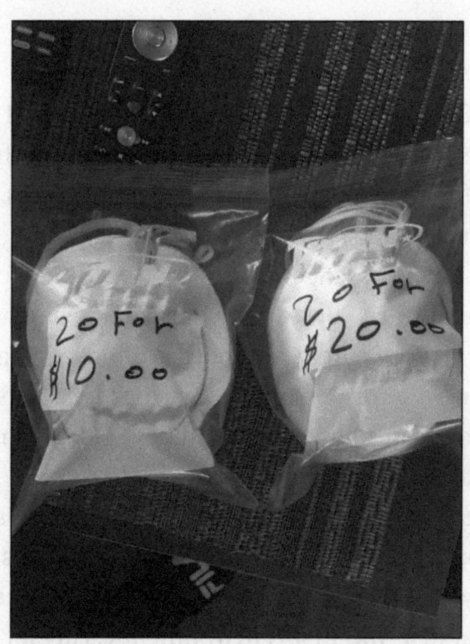

Chapter 44

COVID-19: Caring for others...

AS BUS DRIVERS WE WALK A FINE LINE WITH THE PUBLIC, as we could never, please everyone. To appease one, we frustrate another such as waiting for a passenger, while another needs us to keep moving in order to connect to another Bus.

We regularly have passengers who ride our buses for reasons other than to get somewhere, or to stay out of inclement weather with nowhere to go. Unfortunately, the need to find coping techniques for societal issues or even for personal issues may be a personal thing with no obvious solutions in sight. We should never forget those with special needs as they may not be obvious.

As I have noted before, perhaps more than ever, this is a time when we have no choice but to think of others as their lives depend on our lives... especially as we were dealing with COVID. Society has been so self-centered that in a "me-first" environment caring for others has been viewed as too costly. But it's an attitude of caring for others that will save us!

We are all in this together, and when parts of society suffer it's a reflection on all of us!

Chapter 45

Times of Reflection...

I CAN APPRECIATE IT HAS BEEN A WHILE SINCE I HAVE jotted down events on my bus, and to be honest, I really do not know why. I have had some awesome days, and some not-so-great days as we have coped with issues surrounding COVID 19 on our buses. Everything from; social distancing, the wearing of masks or gloves, to the limit of passengers we are allowed to have on the bus.

We have had passengers complain that we are allowing too many folks to ride, or that we have allowed more than our maximum. Or on the flip side, we have had passengers complain that we are leaving folks standing on the streets as we drive by them. Either way, we cannot win.

I had this one lady scold me because I allowed two more people on my bus than our guidelines suggest. By doing this, it prevented her from having an adequate social distance perimeter. I could have easily pointed out that she was not wearing a mask, but I decided not to. I merely asked her, "of the five passengers who just boarded, how could I have prevented two of them from boarding since it was rear door loading? Or who should I not have allowed on?!" I then continued, "if you feel uncomfortable, you are more than welcome to disembark and take the next available bus behind me if there is room. I am now changing the Bus's status to 'Sorry, Bus full'." She merely replied, "never mind just drive on!"

You know, I've mostly shared heartwarming stories with you, and believe me, there have been many. It is just that, by the time I get home, I am exhausted, and the good stories have taken a backseat to the trying moments and stressful events on the bus.

I still love my job and my interactions with passengers. But we have now been shielded from our passengers with a plexiglass partition, and folks have not been allowed to use our front doors. As such, people do not walk by me anymore. I cannot greet my passengers or thank them for their payment. Our passengers have been restricted to boarding and leaving via the back doors and have not been required to pay for their rides at all for the past 3 or 4 months. I mean at this point, I think we have all lost something, and in terms of customer service we have to adapt. Sadly, as Bus drivers we have lost much of the connection we had with passengers.

But you know, I had this passenger last Saturday who has ridden my bus many times before over the last few years. He reminded me just how special and fortunate I am to be a bus driver.

As we were driving up the road and he was well behind our chained off barrier, and my plexiglass shield, we still managed to exchange pleasantries. He asked me if he could give me a gift. I said, "sure you can, but you really don't need too."

He replied, "I know, but I was thinking about you last Saturday and thought I really wanted to do something special for you!" "Me," I said, "come on stop it, I love what I'm doing, and I do get paid to drive your sorry butt around town!" We shared a brief laugh and he continued, "come on, stop the bus, and let me give it to you!"

Well, as I was about a minute ahead of schedule I thought, sure. In truth, I was also starting to feel a bit awkward, so thought it best to just kind of get this over with. I stopped the bus, opened my shield, and went back to him, still within a safe physical distance. Well, as he's handing me a card, he says, "this is for all the times you've helped me out when I was struggling to find a job and for the countless times, I've seen you help other passengers. You really are special and we're very fortunate to have you!"

I said, "come on, stop it, you're embarrassing me!" He then continues, "you know, I especially remember that time you helped that blind man who was trying to find his transfer stop when he got off your bus! You noticed he was all confused, and you stopped the bus, got out and took him to his new stop. Don't you remember the passengers clapping for you?!" I said, "sure I do, but you were on my bus?!" And he said, "I sure was and have never forgotten!"

He continued, "well, especially now with all this craziness of this virus, you have not changed. I really want you to have this, and please you can't say no!" I humbly took his card and as I looked at it, I was blown away!" It was a Dinner gift card for $100! I said, "are you crazy, or have skipped your Therapy Sessions?! This is way above and beyond. Come on, you can't be serious?!" He said, "I'm dead serious. I really just want to thank you in these crazy times!"

So many things ran through my head. As humbled and as grateful as I was, it was like I was in shock. I gave him a double take as I went back to my seat and said, "are you serious?" He said, "yes, now get back to your work or I'm going to be late for work!" These are very trying times, yet as things change, we cannot forget to be caring and compassionate for one another.

God, I love my job. It affords me the opportunity to meet some awesome people! And yes, I did in fact verify that the card has a $100 value!

Chapter 46

Wearing Masks...

THESE HAVE BEEN TRYING TIMES GIVEN PEOPLE'S RELUCtance to wear masks to help curtail COVID-19. I can appreciate the frustration and nuisance, as it is uncomfortable. I almost lost my hearing aids four times when they fell off while removing my mask. Wham! Almost $5,000 down the drain!

Anyway, I was driving my bus last week, on a weekday to be exact. The lack of folks trying to wear masks was truly disconcerting. Even though it is supposed to be mandatory! At times I counted, and out of 20 riders – a paltry 6 may have been wearing their masks.

Well, this past weekend was certainly refreshing and a complete turnaround in terms of folks trying to wear their masks. In fact, I would say 90-95% were wearing masks when entering my bus.

At one point a group of about eight passengers were boarding, and one young girl was not wearing a mask. I put my hand over my face questioning/reminding her about wearing a mask. She replied that she had one but would put it on in her seat.

I watched as she found a seat directly behind the rear doors and was waiting for her to put her mask on. Well, as we began traveling, I noticed she still had not put on her mask. I would have preferred she had simply been honest and admitted she didn't have one and we could simply move on. I must admit, I felt a bit annoyed, because now folks had to walk directly by her as they left the bus.

Everyone on the bus at that time had a mask on, and I'm certain she noticed, as quite a few gave her a look as they departed. After a while, I could tell she was extremely uncomfortable. No one said anything, and I am certain she learned a valuable lesson with no words being spoken. I just wish it was more of a lesson of caring for others, rather than one of humiliation or of being singled out.

As the day progressed, the numbers remained the same with at least 95% wearing masks, which was awesome for a Sunday, if not any day.

Then there was this young guy in his mid-20's who was boarding my bus with no mask at all just like the young girl earlier. But, when I asked him where his mask was - because some did not have them on but would be carrying one - he simply replied, "I don't have one." I said, "you don't have one?" He said, "nope!" I then asked, "you do realize they are mandatory now eh, and in fact you need one to enter a store or mall, eh?" He said, "yes, guess I'll have to buy one."

As he was waiting for his transfer, I continued "you know, if you don't mind me saying, wearing a mask is not for you, it's for my mother who is 94 now, it's for your grandmother, or someone's 3-year-old child or brother who has asthma. It's a sign you care for others and are not the selfish type. You certainly don't give me the impression that you don't care, but perhaps you just haven't really thought it through."

Well, he took his transfer and simply headed back to his seat. He did not say anything, but you know, when he was leaving, he made sure he got my attention as he headed for the back doors. He smiled while putting his hand over his face and gave me a thumbs up. I really felt that and thought, 'maybe I got through to him.' Wearing a mask is truly a sign of caring for others. Be safe out there, my friends!

Chapter 47

Panhandlers...

NOT THAT MY PERSPECTIVE ON PANHANDLERS IS ANY more valued than yours but having grown up on welfare and in a welfare environment with 'begging all around me', I have quite strong views because of my upbringing.

I learned incredibly young how not to become a product of my environment, or at the very least how outsiders viewed us. At age 16 while in grade 11, I had two jobs. One with Bell Telephone before and after school on certain days; repairing flat tires or slow leaks on their vans. And the other job was at The Terrace (a recreational facility for Ice Skating, Roller Skating and Curling); cleaning and pebbling their Curling sheets... of which they had 18 (the largest in North America). One pay cheque was for me, and the other for my mother.

I resented the stigma of living on welfare and did my darndest to overcome and to hide it. I never wanted anyone to know, and as such worked my butt off to have my own money.

Anyway, this past Saturday it would seem those feelings resurfaced with a few passengers on my bus. First there was a middle-aged lady with about 6 kids in tow heading to a No-Frills grocery store. In my family there was 9 kids, so I knew of adventures of going shopping with mom and the gang.

She looked so stressed, and the look in her eyes reminded me of the look my mother used to have. The kids were not dirty or anything, but I remembered the excitement of anticipation of treats mom just might buy in their eyes. You know, it really touched home for me.

She was standing close to me and asked me how my day was going. I said, "all things considered, not bad given our situation with COVID-19." She said, "tell me about it! I've got my motley crew nonstop now after losing my job, and nowhere to send the kids!" I said, "I can only imagine what it's like as a parent, but my mom was in much the same boat as you, and you know, I can tell your kids love you as much as I love my mother for what she did for us!" My God, she almost started to cry and said, "that has got to the sweetest thing I've heard in such a long time, thank you so much, you made my day." You know something... what an incredible feeling she gave me!

Later, on the same Saturday, there was my 'buddy' who is always either on drugs or drunker than a skunk. Not to mention dirty as hell and with his cane (which others no doubt could view as a weapon). He is in his mid-40's I would say, and always has a story of ailments - such as broken bones or of surgery. And of course, he is always anxious to show off his scars.

Anyway, he got on my bus and was all excited to see me; asking where I have been, and that he was asking around and looking for me. I simply said, "well, you realize I only do this route on Saturdays for now, and then next month it will be only on Sundays." I continued, "so how have you been?" Oh, my goodness, he starts rambling about how he busted up his toe the other night when he went to go pee at 3:00am. He went on about calling 911 for an ambulance, but the Police showed up and gave him a hard time, all the while he was cussing them up. They never took him to the hospital and his toe is still all busted up... all for a pee!

Well, he got off my bus and promised to have a coffee for me on my return trip. I told him, "Please don't worry as I've got my mug, but thanks anyway." I figured he was too high or drunk to remember, but sure enough, there he was with a huge coffee for me. He even admitted someone bought it for him... lol.

Given his huge grin, I simply could bear to hurt him by not accepting it. I know he does not have any money, as I have seen him pan-handling in various locations. Seems the poorer some folks are, the more generous they are. I must admit, I care about him but simply cannot care too much, if that makes any sense. Beneath it all, he truly is a nice guy but is simply struggling to cope.

Then, finally, there is another fellow like my coffee buddy. He always has his old, tattered bike with him. I was excited to see him so I could tell him of how I noticed him last week and of how he had me in stitches. You see, where he was pan-handling, there were two - 'Two Men and A Truck' moving trucks on his corner. He began flexing his muscles with both arms insinuating that they must be strong as hell. Well, he had both crews in their trucks laughing, and me as well!

As he got on my bus, I told him his ride was on me, as I put a Toonie in the fare box. I told him it was because he gave me a good laugh from the week before, and about how he made everyone's day with his antics.

I then told him of the time I was at a Blue Jays game and this guy was pan-handling while wearing an old dirty and tattered Santa Claus outfit. He held a sign that read 'Out of work and Mrs. Claus kicked me out!' I told him that because that guy made me laugh so much, I gave him $10! I then continued, "you've got a good sense of humour, use it and I'm sure folks will give you more than just spare change!"

He smiled and said, "you may be on to something there. I do love making people laugh or smile. I could even bring out my harmonica!" I quickly replied, "sure why not? you are funny when you want to be." He then says, "hey, have you ever seen me ride my bike backwards?" I said, "yes, about three years ago and you scared the heck out of me. I thought for sure you were going down for the count when you left my bus and jumped on your bike backwards and rode down the street!" He began laughing. I then tore off a transfer and added an hour to its duration. I said, "here ya go my friend. Just be careful now and don't forget, folks will give you more money if they feel you've earned it!" To my amazement he said, "yea I know... you're a good man!"

You know, in reflection, it was another awesome day on my bus.

Chapter 48

Bittersweet...

OUR WORK SCHEDULE IS IN BLOCKS CALLED SIGN UP periods. These blocks can range from four weeks to nine weeks. The actual routes we do may vary within what they refer to as crews. In essence, our work may be the same for a 5-day stretch, have multiple days that are the same, or may differ each day.

Well, we have just finished a 9-week period and are about to begin a new period. As such, the relationships we have forged will have to be put on hold, should we not have the same crew on the following sign-up period - which I did not.

This past crew was a nice mix of very residential areas, with a long stretch on a major road. Each route has its nuisances and affect the relationships we forge with our passengers. That is, many times if I have a senior in a walker or if there is a thunderstorm, I will drop them off in front of their house. It is a feel-good moment for other passengers as well, as it reassures passengers that their driver cares.

Anyway, last Friday was my last day on this mixed route/crew, and the love I received was truly heartwarming. First, there was this grandfather taking his two young granddaughters for a walk in their stroller. One was behind the other, and both were around 4 years old. I have seen them before and as they saw me coming up the road the grandfather stopped, and they both began waving with huge grins to me. Normally it is only the girls who wave, but this time even Grandpa was waving and smiling! I slowed down reciprocating and savored the moment.

Later that day there was a young couple near a bus stop in the residential area. One of them was looking confused as she kept glancing at her phone. They were on the opposite side of the street, so I slowed right down, opened my window, and asked them if they were lost. The girl quickly answered "oh no" - a friend was picking them up and was late. She then said, "but my gosh, thank you so much!" Many times, folks get confused with North and South on their phones and since they were right by a bus stop, I thought that may have been the case.

Now, I am at the other end of this long stretch of a major street and this older gentleman is running for my bus while carrying objects packed in his arms. He got on the bus and paid by Presto (a debit type card for fares) but was not sure he was on the right bus. Not able to speak English, he hands me a piece of cardboard; with the route number, multiple bus stops listed, and his destination at the bottom. I assured him with a "yes" nod and then motioned that he could put his stuff on the wheel-well to my right. I was not sure if he understood me, but I then said, "don't worry, I will let you know when we get there as you have a long ride". He was out of breath from running but was still able to express his gratitude as he kept saying "gracias, gracias" as he went and sat down.

I could tell he was still very confused as we began our constant turns in the residential area, but I assured him with hand gestures that he was ok and that I did not forget about him. Once we reached his stop, I called out the stop and with a deep sigh of relief he quickly got up to get his stuff. Then, as he is leaving the bus, he awkwardly puts $5 on my Presto machine which then falls to the ground as he rushes out the front door. I quickly called out to him "hey Senior." He turned back and saw the $5 bill on the ground. He put his stuff down, came back in, and picked it up.

As this older gentleman is handing me the money I said, "please, you don't have to do this it was my pleasure helping you!" As he was insisting, I put my hand out from behind our plexiglass shield and as he places the $5 bill in my hand, he cups my hand with both of his and says, “no senior, it my pleasure, Gracias!”

The day is winding down and another stand out moment occurs...I am on a roll! In the residential area I was driving up to the end of a street and needed to make a left turn. Well, directly in front is a house with two young boys (5-6 years old) with their father on the veranda. Suddenly, the boys started jumping up and down waving at me and wanting me to honk my horn. I must admit that during this signup period I’ve seen them before and exchanged waves as they have been out for walks with their parents, but never on the veranda. Of course, I gave them two honks, and a huge wave and grin from ear to ear.

You know, there are so many rewards being a bus driver. But you know, I relish each passenger who leaves my bus saying, “thank you” or as they walk by the front giving me a wave and smile. I tell you; it makes my day.

I am not merely a ‘Bus Driver’; I’m a ‘Transit Operator’ who simply loves his job as it affords me the opportunity to; play with a big toy, drive, be outside, and care for others. Believe me, there are oh so many issues one can encounter on our buses, but I choose to stay focused on the positive.

Chapter 49

Dealing with Adversity...

WELL, I WORKED THIS PAST CIVIC HOLIDAY, AND HAD A few memorable moments which had me thinking about how we all deal with adversity personally. Many folks truly struggle as they may not have the tools or resources to deal with tough situations. Some due to mental issues, and some may have simply been so devastated that they simply broke emotionally and have given up in this struggle of life.

On my very first trip I was moved by what I saw in a bank which was closed but was where its ATM machines were located. We have a woman who is a frequent 'resident' of one of our terminals and she appears to be homeless. She is always there and is constantly drunk or sleeping. I have personally spoken to her about drinking on transit property, but never called Transit Enforcement. Most recently I saw her sleeping in one of the shelters, and in fact others have seen her urinating in a shelter (prior to our public washroom being built). She is well known among other drivers and all attest that she is harmless and poses no threat to anyone. She is very quiet and keeps to herself. I think she simply wants to be around people but has lost the desire to interact.

Anyway, what moved me was that she was in the closed bank as it was raining and was cleaning. What struck me was her attention to detail as she was meticulous in her cleaning. Obviously taking pride in what she was doing as she was smiling when reviewing her hard work. Immediately I thought she must have had a family at some point which she cared for, as she must be in her mid-50's. For me, this is very sad.

Later that day I had a big burly fellow board my bus with no mask. I merely put my hand over my mouth to remind him a mask is required. His immediate response was, "I don't have one, what are you going to do about it" in a harsh angry tone. I then said, "nothing, it's your issue but you do realize that going into any store or mall, it's now required and it's going to be a constant issue for you. No worries, enjoy the ride." He said nothing and took his seat. Regardless of his issues, it is his own attitude which will make his life a constant struggle. I just hope my non-confrontational attitude and words got him thinking. The rest is up to him.

In the middle of the day, it stopped raining. In one of our shelters along the route was this scruffy man in his early 50's drinking beer. What amazed me was there had to be at least a dozen cans spewed all around the shelter, the same brand that he was drinking. The thing is, they were not merely by the entrance, but all around the shelter. I should have called Enforcement, but it did not even cross my mind as he was not a danger to anyone. He was minding his own business, and as I returned, I thought that I should have probably called it in. As I approached the shelter on the other side, I looked over to see him gone, and the entire area cleaned up of all the beer cans. Anyway, why the need to drink while in a bus shelter? The man is obviously struggling and did not need me to create more issues for him. Or did he... hmm?

Bottom line is, we all have issues we deal with. Let's not lose our compassion or empathy. Life is a struggle and at times we simply must resist being too harsh in our judgment or be too quick to react.

Stay safe my friends!

Chapter 50

A Special Thought...

HAVE YOU EVER HAD A THOUGHT, AND THEN SUDDENLY burst out laughing with no one around?

Well, yesterday I was in my 'zone' driving my bus, when suddenly I visualized the look on my four-year-old grandson's teacher's face as he told her "You give me a headache!"

Now, my Grandson is in JR Kindergarten and is in the virtual stream. As such, my son was with him at home, and he was taken aback with what his son/my grandson said. Indeed, the look on my son's face would have been priceless too!

I could not stop laughing, just simply imagining the startled looks both must have been sharing. My son quickly tried to address the situation and asked my grandson "Lucas, you don't say that! Where did you learn that?!"

My grandson calmly replies, "Pappy says that to me all the time", with a smile on his face.

Now, one must bear in mind... to him it is a joke as I always say it when we are playing, and I am laughing like the goof that I can be.

Kids will say the darnedest things, and so will Pappies!!

I know, I know; this Pappy better watch what he says around his little buddy going forward eh?

One would have thought I learned previously having two young-ins turn out pretty good, eh? Um... nope!

Chapter 51

Remembrance Day Memory...

REMEMBRANCE DAY MEMORIES, AND A SIDE NOTE TO MY stories - sparked by my dear friend Lisa Haley. I will never forget a time I took a Canadian Armed Forces Regiment for practice drills or exercises shortly after they just returned from a tour in Afghanistan during my Coach Bus driving days. This occurred during my days with Coach Canada. Not one person in the Regiment was over the age of 23, yet they all looked over 40! No youthful exuberance or joking around. They sat quietly and seemed to have sadly lost all their innocence. It was a small group of about 20 soldiers who were just completing their tour of duty. One soldier (Adam) still had his hand wrapped in bandages after losing a couple of fingers. He was leaning against a tree smoking a cigar. Adam had introduced himself to me on the Bus, so I felt it was fine to approach him and thank him for his service on a personal level. His reaction humbled me, the morose look on his face began to fade as he smiled and said, "you my friend, are the first to say that." I remember the stories my father told me of his own time in the service (our Canadian Armed Forces – Air Force division), but I will never forget Adam.

Thank you to all who have served!

Chapter 52

Life Events – We Carry On...

WE ALL HAVE HAD HARD AND WHAT SEEM LIKE IMPOSsible events in our lives in which we must deal with... yet we still function, as though all is good. I have not mentioned these events in my stories, but I will describe why... as in the span of two and a half months there have been two major life events in my life which have shook my world. Perhaps you will understand my silence...

The first is with my mother. A couple of days ago I was reminiscing about my older brother Bob (R.I.P.) and about what he meant to me. Well, he meant much more to our mother, being her first.

I do not say that with any reservation as a mother's first born will always be her first. My mother hadn't been well for four years, as she was in Palliative care and bedridden. In fact, a large part of her was lost when my older brother Bobby died... her life energy was just sort of sucked out of her. Of course, she loved the rest of us unconditionally, but she was just never the same after Bobby died (some 20 years ago from Cancer – a brain tumour).

My brother Dominique put it oh so well; in that it was her memories of him that kept her going. Just When we are at our lowest its fond memories which keep us going!

Anyway, I firmly believe that my Guardian Angel - Bobby - helped in relieving Mom of her sorrow and ill health by taking her home where she's wanted to go for years. Mom was very ready to be with him, with my youngest brother Richard (who died of a sudden heart attack just a few short years ago...R.I.P.), and many other loved ones in her immediate family.

My mother (Medea Boucher) died today after years of suffering and in Palliative Care at the age of 92 (I know I sometimes mistake her age for 93). Mom was an incredibly quiet soul who loved and cared for others - asking for nothing in return. Anyone who came into our home with an empty belly left with a full belly and a warm spot in their hearts for her. My mother never spanked me, or for that matter ever yelled at me. I knew how much she loved me and the worst thing I could ever do growing up was to disappoint her.

I really feel she learned how to show her love with a mere look. With her quiet, deep-set eyes and loving heart she inherited from her father, my Pappy and Grandfather. This is the reason I want to be my "Pappy" for my grandchildren as he became my best friend when I lived with them the last year of his life shaving him and listening to his stories of life in British Guyana.

I know this is a bit long winded, but I honestly feel that my oldest brother Bobby and my youngest brother Richard now have 24 hour front row seats with Mom and Dad, as they look down on us.

Thank you, Bobby, for taking Mom home. She surely suffered enough.

R.I.P. Mom. (March 11/28 – Sept 04/20).

Chapter 53

Life Events – We Continue to Carry On...

WE LOST A GEMSTONE OF A MAN WITH THE PASSING OF my ex-father in-law last night. No words properly express my Condolences for all who are now hurting knowing we will never see him or his smile again.

I have known Senhor Antonio since I was about seven years old, and my love will live on forever with memories of his humour and kindness forever etched in my heart. As a role model he marched to his own drummer with humility and compassion for everyone. Although he was 'old school or old country' he always did things in his own unique way. Be it jogging at the age of 70, to making his own wine from grapes, to dancing with a huge grin.

Just think, the man came to Canada from Portugal in the very early 1960's leaving his wife and two very young children to raise money to bring them to Canada for a better life. He worked like hell for three years in the Tobacco fields and even picking worms at night to save money. Finally, he brought my future wife, her brother, and his wife... eventually buying a home and raising his family.

I tell ya, he never missed a Santa Claus parade. I would wager he holds the record for most Santa Clause parades attended in Toronto. Christmas was very special to him. In fact, every Christmas he dressed up as Santa as we stuffed pillowcases in his bed to pretend, he was sleeping. Once, my young son asked "Daddy, why does Santa have a Portuguese accent?" Laughing we told him, "Oh, it was a special visit from the Portuguese Santa to make us feel better about Christmas!"

For me, Senhor Antonio's influence and love of life... not just at Christmas, but for the true blessings of life... and love of family will live on in me for the rest of my life!

R.I.P. Senhor Antonio

Chapter 54

Ramblings on Death...

PLEASE BEAR WITH ME AS THIS COULD BE A LONG ONE.

I am not going to dwell on why this has been a nasty year for me. Surely it has been for many others, too. Suffice it to say, I have found myself rather bitter, depressed, and feeling a bit sorry for myself.

The recent deaths of two extremely close people to me are weighing heavy on my heart. The loss of my mother, and then my father in-law that I knew since I was seven years old, were devastating to me. Even though both were in their 90's, and in the case of my mother, in palliative care for the past 4 years, the pain of these loses is tremendous.

Today my extended heart family, who I have known since I was seven years old, was hurting again as another loved one died. Senhora Alda, my father in-law's sister in-law, was called home. As such, the pain of death that we have been dealing with recently in my heart family continued with the funeral of Senhora Alda. Sure, she was old and ill, but one can never be truly prepared for the loss of a loved one.

As a young kid I vividly remember her loving and caring ways, back then we were all tight and one big family. I was not their blood family, but she made me feel like I was. We worked harvesting crops in farmer's fields, butchered pigs, made tomato and pepper sauces, and even smoked Chouriço. I would have watched the funeral service online today, but alas I was working and driving my Bus.

Ironic, as at one point I was driving by a Cemetery, and I noticed an old lady making her way up the street with the aid of her walker. She was about 200 yards from the stop. I pulled over and asked her where she was going. She immediately came over to my bus and said she had just visited her husband's grave site and wanted to go home, but her stop was on the opposite side of my run. I told her, "If you're not in a rush you can come with me, and I will take you there." As she got in, I explained that I just had to finish the trip I was on, and that we would need to turn around to get her home. She tried to pay, and I insisted it was my Christmas present to her.

Well, near the end I needed to pop into our washroom and told her I would be right back and to not go anywhere without me. She quickly grabbed my hand with both of hers and said, "you are a God send and he is going to bless you and your family, you are such a good man!" It caught me off guard and I said, "my God, no worries he's already blessed me with my grandchildren. You just stay put, and I'll be right back!"

When I returned, I wanted to show her a video clip of my grandson playing and dancing to a toy he has with music. It is only about a minute long and she simply loved it saying, "I can see your spirit in him... God bless you!" Blown away again with her love, we continued as she had just filled my heart with warmth.

I fully expected a detour on the route when I started, as there was a pedestrian fatality the previous night, but the investigative work had cleared by the time I started. Just as we approached the intersection, I noticed a small group of people putting flowers on a pole in remembrance of the deceased pedestrian. I immediately stopped my bus as I was going in the opposite direction and tooted my horn twice to get their attention.

When they looked at me, I made the symbol of prayer and then put my hand over my heart to demonstrate my condolences as I knew what they were doing and that I could feel their pain. Two of them put their hands over their mouths and heart and mouthed the words "thank you."

I continued and worked like hell to hold back my tears as this year has just had so much death for me to deal with.

We finally got down to my older friend's stop and she insisted on clasping my hand one more time, and I felt COVID be damned!

I began thinking of this beautiful old lady and of Senhora Alda, and you know, death has a way of keeping us alive. Both had a special love about them. For some reason, this had me think about my Cousin Jacque's girlfriend that I met at his funeral just a few short years ago. Well, we are now friends on Facebook and out of the blue, she came to my defense yesterday on a post I made on Facebook. It blew me away. I barely know her, yet our connection had her standing up for me. Just think, my cousin's death enabled us to meet and here she is defending me. Amazing.

What made me feel even better, was when my friends on Facebook began defending her when she was rudely addressed. I truly felt blessed that my friends were defending her, who was defending me. All because of a connection derived out of the death of my cousin.

You know, I got home and continued reflecting on death and of its effects on us. I thought that death has a way of making sure we appreciate life even more than normal. For some reason I thought of a dear friend from a previous job with CP Rail and thought, I wonder how she and her young family were holding up in these crazy times?!

Claudine always had a real zest for life and her laughter always lifted my spirits. I have never met her daughter, but Facebook has provided us an avenue to stay in touch and connected, even if not in person. Well, I reached out to her, and our connection was still there as good friends.

She told me she was just about to make dinner. I asked her if she wanted a quick 5-minute cheaters meal. Laughing she said "sure!" I really missed that laugh. She said she was always into quick dinners...lol...and here is my recipe for all to savour. Two cans of Cream of Mushroom Soup and two cans of Tuna. Mix the two with no additives like milk, and then serve over toast. Ta-Da! Dinner in five minutes... lol!

Turns out, she did not follow my advice. and instead settled for some quick wings and fries and some steamed asparagus. However, what really got me was her daughter's contribution to dinner. Christmas Brownies.

You know, life can be crazy. This has been a terrible year overall for me and oh so many others, yet in turmoil there is peace. We can be so down, yet easily uplifted by the right triggers. When seeing my friend's daughter's smile with her Christmas Brownies in a picture, I honestly felt rejuvenated and warm.

I know that in death, there is always something good even though it doesn't feel that way at the time. In the depths of mourning, it can trigger one to appreciate the joys of life.

Thank God for Christmas Brownies and the spirit of Christmas! Thank you, Kayla!

Chapter 55

Train Crossing...

NO DOUBT EVERYONE HAS BEEN FRUSTRATED FOLLOWing a bus which pulls up to a train crossing when they stop and open their doors with lights flashing. Yet, there is no train in sight! But it's the law.

Well, one night the requirement scared the 'bee-gee-bees' out of me!!! It was snowing and extremely late at night, in a very dark area with few lights. I had but one passenger in the bus and it was dead quiet. I was driving what we refer to as an 'artic' which is a 60-foot Articulating Bus; one of the long Accordion looking busses. The pick-up is quite slow, especially when on an incline.

I approached the tracks with my flashers on and as required opened the doors, looked both ways, could not see much between the brush and all the houses, and listened with nothing to prevent me from proceeding across. Anyway, I stepped on the gas and suddenly, the red lights and bells started ringing due to an oncoming train! Holy 'shite!'

Now, being the professional I am - my training kicks in - even though I am panicking. I continued across the tracks, hoping like hell my trainer was right all those years ago. Do not hesitate or stop. Hit the gas and go! Once the bells and lights begin, one has about 15 or 20 seconds before the arms start coming down. This should be enough time to safely cross before the arms come crashing down.

I made safely across and did my trainer proud. Choo-choo be damned...lol! Oh, and proof I am not in need of Depends, so all was fine.

A new day, but back to the same tracks. Today was a bright, mild, and beautiful day. As I approached, I noticed a young family simply waiting by the tracks to see the frequent GO Train which comes by. The family consisted of four young adults a little boy of about four years of age and a baby in a stroller.

I stopped at the tracks and noticed the little boy looking at me. So, I gave my horn a double honk, as I opened my door and waved at the little boy, and everyone waved back. Then, the little boy motions for me to lower my mask. When I did, he began jumping up and down as he must have remembered me from prior crossings.

As much as I wanted to savor the moment I had to continue and gave my little buddy an extra special wave and honk as I closed my doors and continued across the tracks. Sure enough, I could see the train approaching in the distance. What a special feeling to think that little boy remembered me.

All the way to the end of my route, my thoughts were with him as I was reminiscing of past crossings when his mother or father would take him to the crossing to watch the train go by. Then a crazy bus driver would honk and wave at him to try and make his adventure that more memorable. It kind of reminds me of the days I used to take my young son and daughter to the airport to watch the Airplanes land. As luck, and fate, would have it, I saw them on my return trip. They were walking home on the same road, and of course I had to give them another honk. This had them all waving again and had my little buddy jumping up and down with his little arms in the air just for me.

God, I love my job, as these are priceless moments for me. Words simply cannot truly express the feeling.

Chapter 56

New Year's Eve...

DRIVING MY BUS THIS NEW YEAR'S EVE 2020 WAS NOTICE-ably quiet at first, given our COVID lockdown. As such, it afforded me lots of time to reflect on events and what can be described as a terrible year for me personally. But it was not only me who had a terrible year. My son and daughter lost two awfully close grandparents in the span of less than three months.

We have also had much to learn and sustain us with the love and support of our family and friends. A large part though was the energy and youthful innocence of my grandchildren. What a fantastic compensator for loves lost. They say it takes extreme pain to genuinely appreciate extreme joy.

You know, my mother (R.I.P.) used to say, 'Claude, make up your bed. You are the one sleeping in it!' It was her way of telling me that what you sew, you will reap. That we are in control of events in our lives, so make sure our actions are positive to produce positive results.

Boy, that was long winded, eh? But you know, I started thinking of my Grandchildren and my mood turned from gloomy and melancholy, to joyful and uplifted. Then, events on my Bus truly began to reflect my mood and actions.

For example, on a particular trip south a couple of guys were getting off as another bus was stopped at a red light at the intersection I was going through. As our stop was across the lights, I quickly asked, "guys, do you want that bus?" They immediately replied, "yes!" So rather than continuing to the stop, I stopped just past the intersection, and they made the other bus. I then proceeded to pick up a lady waiting at the stop, and she says, "that was awfully nice of you!" I looked at her and said, "yea it was, wasn't it?!" She laughed like hell, even through her mask I could see her eyebrows going up and down.

On the trip back a young teenaged boy came out of his apartment driveway. He saw my bus coming and begins waving at me. I am a fair distance away, so he starts running for the stop. When someone makes an effort, I will do everything possible to assist them if I can, so I began honking for him to stop running and picked him up mid-stop. As be boards, I said "you know, had you simply stood there, I would have driven right by you, but because you made an effort, you earned the ride. Happy New Year, your ride is on us!" He smiles and replies, "good lesson man, my dad says the same thing. Make an effort and good things will happen. Thank you and Happy New Year!"

I am on a roll here, eh? Anyway, later a young girl of about 14 gets off my bus and begins sanitizing her hands with a small bottle of hand sanitizer. But it is almost empty, and she begins whacking the heck out of it. I just happened to have a small new bottle in my pocket, so I opened my door and shield, and called out to her to get her attention. As she looked at me, I said, "catch" as I tossed it to her. Surprised, she dropped her bottle and caught it! As she smiled, I said, "Happy New Year!" and closed my door to drive off into the sunset as it was getting dark.

What a day/night it was turning out to be. All because of the mood my grandchildren put me in and my mother's words of wisdom. Later, a guy is walking up the street far from a stop. I guessed that he may want my bus, so I tooted my horn and gestured if he wanted a ride. Given his reaction when he got on the bus, one would think I saved his life. He came running over and began to thank me over and over as he boarded.

You know, it was an awesome shift after all. Here I was moping about what a terrible year this has been. Sure enough, my mother's words rang true. 'You make your bed, you sleep in it,' combined with the love and inspiration of my grandchildren is going to make next year one awesome year.

Happy New Year folks!

Whatever inspires you will guide you. Trust Pappy!

Chapter 57

Communication Is the Key...

MISCOMMUNICATION OR THE LACK OF COMMUNICATION has been at the root of problems or missed opportunities for our entire lives. No different than when I am driving my bus.

Just the other day I was driving at dusk and picked up some passengers. I scanned the intersection to see if it was safe to proceed and noticed an old man waiting to cross, he was on my left. The coast is clear, and my light was green, so I proceeded. The old fellow begins waving at me. It is cold and I am a minute and a half ahead of schedule, so I decided to wait for him on the other side of the street. Excited, the old man notices and begins crossing to get to the same side I was on now.

Good golly, the light took forever to change, and by the time he got to me, I was now three minutes behind schedule. As he got on the bus, he was grateful as the poor guy was freezing. I told him he was more than welcome. To be honest, if I knew how long the light would take to change, I would not have waited, as I had 15 odd passengers trying to make connecting buses.

We continued for a while and at another intersection a lady in her early thirties came running from another bus which had just crossed the same intersection. She got on in a hurry and began scouring through her bag for her Presto card. She was holding on and secure, so I proceeded down the road. Now she's struggling to find her card and says, "my God, I can't find my wallet!" I said, "no worries, take your time." Panicked, she replied, "oh no. I left it on my seat in the other bus!" I replied, "are you sure?" And she said, "yes, and when I saw you, I rushed out without putting it back in my bag!"

At this point various things can happen, as everyone can imagine. I told her, "Well, hopefully it's turned in to the driver and they will put it into the lost and found." The poor girl is distraught now almost to the point of tears and says, "my God, what else could go wrong today, it's been a disaster so far!!!"

I began to explain the process to her and to be optimistic about it. I advised her to call our customer service line to inform them of the situation and that hopefully she may get it back in a couple of days. I thought to myself, 'poor thing's got a 65% chance of getting it back.'

Then I thought I should call in to see if Control can contact the other bus immediately. I pulled my bus over and called our dispatchers/controllers. I gave our dispatcher the details and suggested that she call the other bus immediately as she may catch the Bus before it reached the Terminal. I hung up and tried to reassure the young lady that things should work out and to have faith, as we continued.

She went and sat down still terribly upset and distraught. I was really hoping things would turn out for this young lady. Well, before I even reached my terminal, I got a call back from Control...our dispatcher!

The wallet was found on the other bus. And the dispatcher/controller told me that the driver immediately walked it over to the office at the terminal. I called for our passenger to come up to the front of the bus. As she is making her way up, she was already on the phone with our customer service giving them the particulars about her wallet, and she had just been told that it was in fact found and turned in! All in all, an awesome turn of events for the young passenger.

She got off the phone with Customer Service and I advised her to get off the bus... cross the street as that Bus would take her to our Lost and

Found at the Terminal it was headed for. She was skeptical she would make it before the office closed, but I encouraged her and off she went.

Now, I do not know exactly how this story ends, but I think it is safe to say it ended well. You know, today topped off two awesome courses of events.

Remember the old man we waited for? Well, he was now the last passenger to get off my bus. He shuffles up to me and says, "you were very special today, we need more people like you in these crazy times, thank you!"

Sure, we have lots of problems driving our buses, but my God I love my job!

Chapter 58

Positive Vibes All Around on a Sunday...

GIVEN ALL THE NEGATIVITY SURROUNDING COVID, THE last thing I expected was a day of nothing but positive vibes. I was honestly expecting the usual loaded bus with folks simply ignoring the requirements of keeping their masks on and of my requests...it was a nice surprise indeed that most were in fact pleasant. Passengers immediately responded to my reminders. When I checked in for work, the bus I was assigned was not one of my favorites. Yet, for some reason, I did not mind. Driving non-stop for eight-and-a-half hours with no rest or breaks longer than a few minutes at any time is tough at the best of times. You can imagine how difficult this becomes if we do not have a break for up to 9 hours!

The weather was bright but overcast enough to soften the glare of the sun. A huge part of prepping for my day is psychologically preparing myself for my assignments, and today was a mixed bag of four different routes. It is almost as though my crew was designed to tie up loose ends for the Scheduler of our work assignments. But you know, I really do not mind it because it affords variety.

A fellow driver started my day off just right. As I handed him the car keys to our relief car, he said, "it's always a pleasure seeing you, and not just because you're relieving me!" Then as I began driving my routes it just seemed that no matter what negative situation arose, I was met with a positive response. Like the lady talking loud on her phone so that the entire bus was forced to listen. I did not want to embarrass her by telling her to lower her voice and to use her inside voice, but I noticed she had dropped her mask. At a stop I got out of my seat and had everyone's attention. I put my hand on my face and seven folks who dropped their masks got the message and raised their masks up, even the lady talking loudly... lol.

Later, I had a couple in their mid-forties who appeared to be on a date board my bus for a few stops. Their giddiness made me smile and I hoped their date worked out for them. On my trip back, the same couple boarded my bus. The guy has an ice cream sundae in a cup, while she had an ice cream waffle cone. Notable to me, was they didn't have napkins. I mentioned to them, "I'm really sorry but you won't be able to eat your ice cream on the Bus as you've got to keep your masks on, perhaps you'd like to wait for the next bus?" She then replied, "oh no that's ok we're only going a couple of stops and won't eat."

As they sat down, I figured she was going to have a mess as her cone would begin to melt. So, I said, "I've got some napkins if you'd like?" She says, "that would be great, thanks!" Sure enough, three stops later they got off and the guy says, "thanks so much for the ride and napkins, have a great day!"

I am now on my final route. I start off at one of our main terminals and do a trip north. After that, I have to do a 'dead head' (a trip with no passengers) back to the same terminal and then do my final trip of the day going north. In essence, on my trip south I am Not-in-Service, as it is three minutes less in terms of run time.

I know the scheduler had their reasons for the 'dead head', but I hate leaving folks waiting for a bus when I can easily pick them up and give them a ride. Therefore, I called in to our dispatch and asked permission to stay in service on my trip south rather than 'dead heading' to ensure my butt is covered legally.

The dispatcher always grants permission, but on this occasion sends me a message on our onboard computers. Now, in my eight years of driving, I have never received a personal message. The message simply blew me away as it was a personal compliment thanking me for being compassionate towards our passengers for staying in service (thank you Janice Camilleri – one of our quality Supervisors)!

With my ego still sky high I am about to do my final trip North before my weekend starts. I am heading up and this young fellow gets on my bus, and it is a new friend I met about a month and a half ago on this very route. He got on and is all excited to see me as he had some awesome news, he wanted to tell me.

I am certain his name is Patrick, and he began to tell me that since he met me, he has had nothing but good luck. He got a solid job in a warehouse, and another part-time job in a FreshCo, both remarkably close to the new apartment he found. He was happy to report that things have really turned around for him. He went on to say that he's taken my advice and encouragement to heart and really cleaned up. All I really did was listen to him and spoke to him as though he was my son. He is a good person who was obviously at a crossroads in his life. We have all been there. I merely removed some of the smoke which blinds us when we are in a storm or fire.

As he is leaving the bus, he asked if he could take a selfie with me. I said sure, but instead makes a very short video with the two of us. With my mask on, I am simply smiling with my eyes and giving a thumbs up. He says on the video, "this is Claude, as in close the door. The bus driver who turned my life around by simply caring."

My God, how can I not love my job!!!

Chapter 59

Folks Are Frustrated, and Their Behaviour is Changing...

IT IS OBVIOUS THE EFFECTS OF OUR COVID MEASURES and requirements, or at least a lack of clarifying the need for positive proactive measures, are taking a toll on folks. And believe me, it has been most prevalent over the past six months.

I noticed this one clean cut fellow waiting at the bus stop smoking a cigarette. He was about to board the bus; he butts out his cigarette on the ground and I could not help but notice he did not have a mask at all. As he boarded the bus I said, "excuse me bud," as I put my hand over my face to reflect a mask is required. He ignored me and continued walking. I repeated in a louder voice, "excuse me buddy," as he is now past me and he stops to look at me. I put my hand over my face again and he replies, "I have a medical condition," in an irritated tone. I smiled and gave him a thumbs up saying, "no problem," as we are not permitted to verify the claim. Meanwhile I am thinking "sure buddy, smoking a cigarette and you can't wear a mask?!"

Late in the day a fellow gets on the bus with his McDonald's happy meal! A large fry, a burger, and a pop. He is fine though, as he is wearing a mask and although passengers are required to always keep their masks on, bringing food items or drinks are permitted. Despite knowing full well what they're going to do. In fact, we even have automated announcements on the bus reminding passengers to not remove their masks for any reason, including, of course, eating.

Anyway, the guy gets on and goes to the back of the bus when he promptly took off his mask and began chowing down. I can clearly see what is going on, but merely tried to ignore it to not escalate an issue needlessly!

On many occasions during our shifts folks come on the bus with their mask on, but as soon as they pass me and sit down, they drop their masks well below their noses. Well, today I had a fellow drop his mask and began talking on his phone. He was not talking loudly, but because he was in the middle of the bus everyone could follow and hear his conversation. Believe me, it is frustrating listening to a whiny drunk person. At one point, he came to the front to put an empty can of Red Bull into the garbage bin. I used the opportunity to remind him to keep his mask on. He says, "yea-yea," and rather than go back to his seat, he went all the way to the back of the bus. I thought, well, at least I would not have to listen to him. It is frustrating, but our hands are tied.

I was at a red light at a busy intersection with a right turn lane beside me, having already dropped and picked up passengers at the stop. A young fellow who appeared higher than a kite and had his pants below his butt was crossing the street from left to right smoking a cigarette. He motions to me that he wanted to board the bus. But, with an open lane of traffic immediately to my right, we cannot and are not permitted to open our doors. I tried using hand signals and even dropped my mask so he could read my lips, but to no avail. He was angry that I would not open my doors and took it personally. I tried to signal him to simply cross the street and I would pick him up on the other side. After several hand gestures - he is now swearing at me and giving me the naughty finger.

Anyway, rather than wait for the light to turn green he runs across the red light and dodges cars as he is running. Once the light changed, I got to the stop and figured at least now I can explain to him why I could not open the doors. Well, he wants no explanation and simply begins calling me names and swearing profanities as he goes to the back of the bus.

Not being a threat to any of my passengers or me, I simply felt it best to leave him alone as he had already done a great job embarrassing himself to those witnessing his behaviour. He sits down and behaves himself once he got it out of his system. As he leaves though, he yelled several other things to me before actually exiting the bus.

It is frustrating having rules which we are not permitted to enforce. But it is probably a good thing because we are alone in the Bus, with no immediate support or back-up.

Now, do not get me wrong. I love my job. There are many times it is just so frustrating as most of us do our part in protecting others by obeying the rules. But at the time we had to continue wearing masks for a longer period simply because others are not following the rules and guidelines. Some people simply do not seem to care or do not believe any of this was real as it's becoming more and more difficult to validate "truths" these days.

Chapter 60

Mean Bus Drivers...

THE BAD OR NEGATIVE THINGS ALWAYS SEEM TO STAND out, right?! Yet, good deeds seem to get lost or overlooked.

A supervisor was helping me yesterday as the Presto unit on my bus was not working (our debit card specialized for transit). I have a particularly good relationship with this supervisor (Rob Shorrock). We actually worked together years ago for the same Coach company (Coach Canada). Our mutual experiences and shared knowledge are very special and similar. I decided to tell him one of my stories, as this Presto issue reminded me of a unique situation.

I told him of an experience I had with a passenger who I asked to leave the bus. It is rare, but this fellow just pushed too many of my buttons. Now, nine times out of ten, the passenger who wants to be last getting on the bus always seems to have an issue or no funds. Well, this young fellow in his late twenties was carrying; a brand-new soccer ball, a shopping bag, a slushy drink with a straw in it, and a cell phone in his other hand with his Presto card.

The fellow boards the bus and says to me, “there is no money on my Presto.” I then said, “no worries find a Loonie and I’ll put you down as a

Senior." On weekends Seniors ride for $1. He then says, "I don't have any money." Not believing him as he's drinking his slushy I said, "come on, you no doubt have something right, even 25 cents? You have obviously been shopping and you are drinking a slushy, now you're telling me you don't have any money? What does that say of your respect for our system just to pay your fair share?" He says "ya, I've got another city's monthly pass but no cash on it."

I guess I caught him a bit off guard, as he pulled out his wallet and says, "I just don't have any change" as he shows me a $5 bill and other bills in his wallet. I then said, "well, since the cash fair is $4, you're only putting an extra dollar... no big deal." He then says, "seriously you're going to charge me extra?!" I replied with, "look at all of these other passengers, they've all paid their fair share... do you seriously expect them to pay and not you? Come on buddy." He then says, "are you going to give me a free ride or not?" I said, "no, you have money but are refusing to pay. Either slip in the $5 or leave the bus." He left the bus, and all is fine. That is until I am questioned should he phone or email a complaint.

You know it is rare that I get so anal on my bus, but the complete sense of entitlement can be a bit much at times. I cannot begin to tell you how many passengers we let ride for free or with only a partial fare or an expired transfer. Especially when the passenger is honest and trying their best. I know it is a simple fare, but it is also the principle and lesson everyone on the bus was witnessing. He was cocky, smug, and just expected a free ride.

Once the fellow left and we continued, four passengers came up to thank me. Such positive responses to the way in which I dealt with our young rider. Some even mentioned the respect I showed him despite asking him to leave. Thus, in the end, it was his ultimate choice and decision. In good form, my supervisor glibly replies, "just be careful eh, I'd hate to hear you got cold-cocked! Just keep up the good work and let them ride, it's just not worth it!"

Ah, the life of a Bus driver. Any different than what appears to be tough love from one's own parent or wife?

Chapter 61

Thoughts as I Prepare to Work This Canada Day...

I AM CANADIAN, AND NOTHING WILL EVER CHANGE THAT. No different than my last name or blood lines passed down by my father and mother. Sure, I could legally change my last name, but no blood transfusions can ever change my bloodlines. As my French-Canadian father always said, "I was born a Canadian, and 'mon esti' I will die a Canadian!"

We are learning of extremely dark and horrendous events which were used to shape our Country. All of which is extremely disturbing to say the least. Is that any different than deep dark secrets being revealed of my father or mother's past? Would they change the makeup of my blood? Of course not!

You know, my father was incredibly well liked and had tons of friends. But, as a father, well, let me just say I used him as a role model of what not to be as a father...despite the invaluable lessons he taught us growing up! In my younger days I simply did not understand him and would avoid him at all costs. However, because of my mother's unwavering and unconditional soft love I grew and matured and learned of the "whys."

No different than what is happening with Canada right now. The good and the bad.

Everything I experienced and learned taught me to be the father I always needed and wanted. No different than the good and bad of what makes us Canadian. We should not hide and run from our Country's deep dark secrets with Indigenous Canadians. We simply cannot sweep them under the rug or remove the tombstones.

Our Country's government knew what was going on. The Church bodies involved all had a hand in the atrocities. All those responsible must bear accountability. I am not about to jump ship because we are learning of even more dark secrets of our Country.

We have got to learn and grow from the mistakes, not turn our backs on them or pretend they never happened. We need our government and the Churches involved to accept responsibility as damaging as it is.

My family was and is far from perfect, and I have never pretended it was any other way. My God do I love my family. As with my Country, this is an opportunity to make our Canada better because of what we are learning.

My Country is akin to my parents. Sure, they made mistakes, but the love, compassion, and understanding made me the person I am today.

My Country is hurting right now, and I am not about to turn my back on it. Instead, let us learn from mistakes and make it better than ever before.

Happy Canada folks. Every child matters!

Chapter 62

Passengers Reflect... Sunday...

IT WAS ABOUT 4:30 PM AND MY BUS WAS SURPRISINGLY quiet for a weekday afternoon. I looked in my rear-view mirror at my crowded bus and the faces of my passengers, each face telling a different story. I found myself reflecting and getting lost in their stories as I was interpreting their personal stories in my mind.

I began thinking of how we all share the same types of emotions, issues, and situations. The only real difference is likely how we react to the trial and tribulations of life. Suddenly, as I was in this reflective trance, a passenger jerked me out of it by saying, "hey, so good to see you, do you remember me?" Startled I said, "no, sorry you'll have to help me out."

Smiling, he replied "it was just this past Sunday, and you blew me away at how you handled such a busy bus with so many things going on! In fact, I've been meaning to call in to your Customer Service to commend you. As crazy as it was with the two mothers with crying children in their strollers, the two seniors with walkers, and that one blind fellow with his dog, you made everyone feel part of a team as you had us caring and helping each other."

I said to the fellow, "oh my God, now I remember you. You got up and gave your seat to that blind fellow, and in fact raised one of the benches for one of the mothers!" He replied, "yea, but only after you asked one of the kids to help raise the other bench in a very positive way which made the kid feel good as he willingly gave up his seat. You had me feeling good too. I could help as well when you thanked me for moving."

I then said to my friend, "ya it was a good bus." He then continued, "you had everyone listening so intently to your instructions and then the story of your grandchildren and of how blessed they make you feel. You compared them to icing on a cake, which was so memorable. That young mother simply loved your story. Did you notice how many times she waved at you when she left? You really made her day!" I said, "I noticed her wave and smile, but was focused on driving as we pulled out. But that makes me feel awesome if I made her day."

Well, it just seemed as suddenly as my friend boarded my bus, he had to take his leave and depart. But, as he left, I said to him, "don't worry about having to call in, you just made my day by reminding me of this past Sunday and of how I helped folks feel good. It truly was an awesome set of events we all shared!!!" He nodded and said, "it sure was - see you again soon!"

To think I left such a positive impression on him made me feel great. Luckily for me, this theme continued. On another trip, an old fellow got on my bus and says, "hey, nice to see you again. It's been so long." I started laughing and said, "you know, you are the second passenger today who remembers me, but I'm at a loss. I'm so sorry, who are you?" I said jokingly.

He says, "it must have been about six months ago, but I clearly remember you letting a young kid on when he only had a Loonie, and you even gave him a transfer! You said to him, "happy birthday you just turned 65, just don't tell my Boss or your mother" I said, "Oh yes, I use that line a lot as it helps in those situations." He continued, "well I thought it was great!" I said, "well, thank you so much my friend. Remind me when I can give you a birthday transfer!" As we both laughed.

Now, both of these passengers had me feeling great. Reflection is a good thing, indeed. Well, most days... lol.

Chapter 63

Sunday, Part 2... 'Threaten my passengers will ya!'

THE SUN WAS SHINING, AND IT WAS SIMPLY GORGEOUS. I started my day at the south end of the route and drive through a residential area. Now, some of you may recall my little friends who wave to me along the way. Sometimes from the railroad tracks or at the little parks around the area. Sure, enough there is one of my little buddies and his parents are waving as I got closer to them at one of the parks. What an incredible feeling for Bus drivers.

The father even struggled to keep him contained as he was bouncing in his arms with excitement. Well, I had to give him a proper greeting. I stopped my bus, gave a little honk, then decided to open my doors and remove my mask to give them a proper smile. This understandably started the little guy temporarily, but his adorable smile quickly adorned his face once more. There is no amount of money to put value to this. It is simply priceless!

Then later in the day, there was another fellow with his two kids leaving the soccer field. They were quite far away, but the father noticed me coming down the road and alerted his children. They all began waving and running, but I had already passed them. I thought, I'm not letting them down! I stopped my bus, honked my horn as I opened my door and waved. They rewarded me by waving more emphatically. What an incredible feeling.

I just picked up about 25 passengers from a mall as it was closing for the day. The bus was packed and loud, with babies in the front crying and folks talking away. It was loud, with no discernible conversation. Sort of like loud white noise. After about ten stops a young girl in her early thirties was getting off, but purposely came to the front doors.

She alerted me to the fact that there was a guy in the very back corner of the bus threatening to kill passengers wearing a green sweater. I asked her for specifics, and she told me he was saying things like 'go back to your own country, you should be speaking English, I'm going to cut your tongues out if you don't shut up, I will kill you mother f*ckers and cut your throats!' I said, "not on my bus," and then another woman came up and verified the situation.

I immediately called into our Control office and alerted them to send support and the Police. They asked for a description, but I could not see or hear him. I said I will call back when possible as I knew it was time to clear my passengers off the bus.

I quickly made an announcement, "sorry folks we have a mechanical issue and need everyone to clear the bus until maintenance arrives! It won't be long, but please stay on the grass as they will be here shortly." I didn't want to alarm anyone, especially the guy in the back. In fact, I was hoping he would find a seat on the grass as well.

As we are all out on the grass, the gambit of emotions rushing through me is mixed, but I reassured my passengers quietly that it would not be long, and our problem would be resolved shortly. More passengers began telling me of the guy in the green shirt sitting by himself and of his threats. I phoned Control on my cell phone, but they were too busy to answer as would not recognize the urgency my call from my cell phone!

About 10 minutes later, the first of two Supervisors arrived and began relaying information to our Control (yep, Rob was one of them). Then wham, four Police cars arrived. No lights or warning and our supervisors quickly approached them to identify the man that was making threats.

They quickly surrounded him and handcuffed him. They had him in the back seat of their car in no time!

I was so relieved as my/our priority was/is to keep passengers safe. Our course of action is to always de escalate an issue to protect everyone! Safety is always a priority and faking a mechanical problem certainly helped diffuse a tense situation!

The Police got their man and began taking statements from passengers who were all extremely relieved and cooperative. As we were all still mulling about, the following scheduled bus came and the passengers thanked me profusely, and they were certainly happy to be on their way with an exciting tale to tell their friends and family!

All in all, that first girl will forever be etched in my memory as she chose the right opportunity to warn me, without alarming the guy. (Thank you, Simone)!

Who said all Sundays are quiet? What a day I had!

Chapter 64

Another Full Day for Me...

SOME TREPIDATION TODAY AS THIS WAS THE FINAL DAY of this route for me. A new crew period was beginning. I really enjoy this particular route as it has a mixture of residential, commercial, and industrial areas to service. Quite the mix. I started off by the Airport and thoroughly love seeing families park their cars to watch the planes coming and going. It takes me back to when I used to do that when my kids were young, and they loved it. Now I know my son loves doing it with his sons and family.

At times folks are so focused with watching the planes land and take off, that they forget all about my bus, and then frantically come running for me. The looks on their faces are hilarious as I leave them in my dust! Just kidding! Up in that neck of the woods is a young friend I met a couple of years ago, and he works up there. He is a foreign student, all alone with no family here. He just completed his bachelor's degree. And now he is concentrating on getting his Permanent Resident card, a requirement for him to stay in Canada (you may remember him as he gave his winter coat to a homeless fellow).

Any father would be oh so proud of him. Many nights he would be leaving or going to work with this huge book, all the while studying while on route. Such a good young kid, but with the compassion of a seasoned veteran who has witnessed many hardships. Anyway, I told him that I wished him well, but that it will be a while until I see him again as this was my last day on this route. Well, crazy as this may sound, our paths keep connecting. Since he has moved a couple of times, he keeps getting on my bus on different routes. This is a passenger who has gained my respect and now I am lucky to call him a friend. I know our paths will cross again. Well, I surely hope so!

For a Sunday, it is busy as usual with families out shopping and enjoying their outings. I have befriended a young family who travel frequently up and down this route. This time Papa is not with them, but the smile on their faces is enough to brighten anyone's day. We have never really spoken due to our language barrier and circumstances, but our connection is very positive and mutual.

The parents are in their late forties if not early fifties. The son is still a student and in his late teens. The daughter is perhaps 11 or 12. The son and mother have no reservations in showing their happiness in seeing me, as they are comfortable with me due to being a regular fixture. But the daughter has always been very shy and reserved. Well, today she was all smiles and was probably the happiest to see me. In fact, even as they left my bus she kept smiling and waving to me as they left for their connecting bus. I sort of felt sad, as I could not communicate with them that I would not be on this route for a while.

As fate would have it, later in the day Papa boards my bus alone. I told him that I had his family earlier and that it was sad, but that I was leaving this route for a while. I told him, "Who knows, but perhaps I might get this route again." He smiles and says, "we hope So, you are my children's favourite driver." As with all bus drivers experience, our paths will cross again.

Then comes my buddy who pan-handles frequently and is quite the character. He is scruffy looking and often has his bike and either harmonica or guitar with him. His outgoing personality can be intimidating to some, but he is always friendly. This is unusual for most panhandlers I have met, as they tend to be very subdued.

Anyway, he takes up residence just behind the back doors, and sets up his possessions around him. There is a young fellow behind him in the back of the bus. I noticed my buddy get up to grab a cup that an earlier passenger discarded. He goes right to the back of the bus and opens a window. As he does this, the young fellow who was in the back moves and comes to sit near the front of the bus. Not knowing what was going on, I kept an eye on my buddy.

A short time later as I lost track of him due to being focused on my driving. He comes up to the front of the bus holding the lid of the cup on tightly. He says to me, "hey buddy, didn't want to startle the passengers, but I've got a wasp in the cup, let me know when you can open the doors!" Stunned. I said, "hell ya, now's a good time!!!" I said to him, "you never cease to amaze me, you seriously saved my bus!" He smiles and says, "hey, for you, anytime" as he goes back to his seat. Crazy, but I am going to miss him as we change crews.

Now I'm on my final run and it's been 8 1/2 hours of driving without any breaks, and I am tired. Sure, we have five- or six-minute layovers, but no discernible break, as such. In any event, a fellow in a wheelchair has completed his grocery shopping and I am picking him up for the second time today. He gets on and we began chatting. Turns out we lived in the same area some 20-25 years ago and we began reminiscing of the area. It just seemed fitting given my thoughts of leaving this route and of passengers I will be missing, if only to be reunited later.

Our life is a journey, and our paths are unexplainably connected as we keep moving forward.

Chapter 65

Behind the Scenes...

WE RECENTLY HAD SOME MAJOR CHANGES TO OUR schedules to make our service more efficient. However, things did not quite go according to plan.

On a given weekday, a typical shift on this route includes seven round trips. The scheduling changes made to make it more efficient included increasing the round trips from 7 to 8! This is accomplished by cutting drive and layover times at the ends. Even driving non-stop, it was still impossible to be on time. Ironically, we kept falling further behind with each trip. These changes created far more problems for everyone. The goal of increasing efficiencies and services for our passengers was simply not being met. I decided to send out a few emails to the higher-ups that work behind the scenes. Other drives provided the latest trip time numbers, as they were very grim and did not have their intended effect to say the least as passengers and drivers alike complained and were frustrated!

The company reversed the changes when they realized the effects of their changes and as such reduced the round trips from eight to six-and-a-half, as well as modifying other crews beginning at different times on the same route. Incredible! Bottom line is our company listened to its workers and passenger complaints realizing they made a mistake and fixed the problem!

I cannot factually say what went on behind the scenes, but I do know that the emails I sent to our Union Executive and Supervisory Staff were forwarded to those of influence with their notes of support. The support the drivers received from our supervisors was truly heartwarming. Our route Supervisors and even our Training departure really went to bat for us as they were and are well aware of the service interruptions.

Never before (that I am aware of), has a transit company modified its schedule midstream to correct a mistake they inadvertently made. This, my friends, is one of the reasons I chose to work for my company. They may be a pain at times, but they need factual data and analytics in which to properly schedule their routes.

There are far too many drivers who go like hell to meet times for a myriad of reasons; could be to simply prove they are good drivers and are doing their best for the company, for passengers to meet other buses, for fear of falling behind scheduled times, and for fear of looking bad. As such, the company looks at these metrics and assumes it can be done. There are...like in any company, the dodgers, who simply do not care or are trying to rack up some overtime. Bottom line is - it all sends false messages and metrics to the schedulers.

Well, kudos to the company for fixing a major problem. However, as you might imagine, they implemented changes to the weekdays, but not on the weekends. As drivers, we are well aware of our scheduled work, but our dispatchers were not made aware of the amendments to our weekend work.

This past weekend I was running further and further behind. When I called in to report my situation, confusion ensued as the other two drivers doing the same route but were on schedule. I was questioned on the radio and in fact, they sent out a supervisor to meet with me personally for an explanation. I was livid, as even he was under the impression that our weekend work was modified. A case of the left hand not communicating with the right hand, to say the least.

Once I made him aware of the situation, he was extremely apologetic and in fact embarrassed. He knew the type of driver I am and of my consistent conscientious work ethics. I am certain the new dispatcher was spoken to, and all is good now. In retrospect I do not take it personally! It will however be interesting to see what happens with our weekend work schedule going forward.

Sure, it takes time to implement change, but why was the weekend work not addressed?! Then I thought, perhaps it was because my email addressed weekday work, and not weekend work? Could it be they are very narrow minded and specific to a task at hand...hmm? lol

You know, I still think my company is the best Urban Transit company to work for. It is certainly not perfect, but this whole issue and incident merely validated my choice to work for this company.

Chapter 66

We Try Not to Assume or Judge, But...

TODAY'S ROUTE WAS A VERY SHORT ONE IN A STRICTLY residential area with lots of turns. I now know what it feels like to be a yoyo. Up and down, and around and around with many turns.

This adventure started with a mother and her daughter. The daughter asked me to confirm where the bus was going, so I confirm the route with her. She said, "oh good, sorry we are new to Canada." I said, "no worries, welcome!" I handed them two free transfers. The young girl explained to her mother in their language, and she nervously thanked me with an extremely strong accent.

Well, we got to the terminal and the few who were on the bus got off. As the new riders got on, a man yells out, "hey, someone forgot their phone" and he brought it up to the front. As he was walking up, a young couple quickly said, "oh, it belongs to that mother and daughter who just got off the bus!" The young fellow then runs like hell to catch the mother and daughter, but my view was hidden by another bus so I could not see the interaction of him returning the phone. He returned elated and feeling great about his good deed. I said, "hey buddy, that's your good deed for the week!" He then says, "ya, man it feels good!"

Anyway, now I am thinking of how various cultures and communities can truly care for one another and get along as they were of different cultures. About 10 stops later, I picked up a lady and as she entered, she said that she thinks she left her phone in this bus and was wondering if anyone had turned it in. ***Gulp*.** The bus went silent. I said, "sorry no, but you're more than welcome to go and have a look." So many thoughts ran through my head hoping like hell she would find her phone. Well, suffice it to say she did not. I knew there was no point in mentioning what happened. As it was best to keep things simple for fear of things escalating into a whole debate and confrontation. Nevertheless, no one said a word as all the eyes were on her.

Anyway, she came back to the front, and I said, "at this point the best thing to do would be to phone our customer service and hope someone turns it in." She says, "I sure hope so, but I doubt it!" As she leaves, the bus is still dead silent. Now, my thoughts were of the guy who gave it to the mother and daughter. Having his thoughts of a good deed come crashing down and transcending into guilt.

Quite a twist, but in the end one can only hope and assume that in the confusion of it all, the mother and daughter may have nervously accepted the phone. I feel quite certain that the mother returned the phone in the end.

One can hope and believe. Besides, my gut told me they were good people. Regardless, this was a whirlwind of emotions!

Chapter 67

A Lost Soul with the Weight of the World on Her Shoulders

THIS PARTICULAR SATURDAY WAS UNUSUALLY VERY quiet. In fact, on this particular route only two buses were scheduled, and as such the interval was about half an hour between the two. I was heading southbound when I noticed a young girl in her mid 30's looking very confused while at a stop. I stopped to allow her in, but she hesitated and was not sure if she should board the bus. I assured her that it was fine to board, hoping I would be able to help, or offer directions.

Turns out she was on the wrong side of the street, going in the wrong direction! I explained the situation to her and advised that since she had just missed her bus going in the direction she needed, she may as well stay with me and have a seat where it was warm.

She agreed and stayed onboard. As I noted earlier, she still looked out of sorts, and I asked her how she was doing as she still looked very confused. She came beside me, and we began chatting. She introduced herself as Sharmi and told me of how she was very new to Canada and very unsure of her future. She was heading to her Immigration Lawyer's office for the first time. I tried to reassure her that things would work out as long as she stayed focused and did not give up on her goals.

Before we reached her destination, I asked her if she knew how to get home. Again, she was not sure, so I told her the quickest way home once she left her appointment. Well, we arrived, and we said our farewell as I wished her luck. As fate would have it, over an hour later on my next run, there was Sharmi across the street going in the wrong direction! The poor girl was so wrapped up in the storm in her life, that simple directions were forgotten or misunderstood.

I stopped and honked my horn to get her attention! Once she recognized it was me, she came running. I am sure she was happy to see a familiar face. Although the route I was driving was a bit longer than the original route I shared with her, I would still be able to get her to the required transfer point she needed.

We began our trek and she stayed by my side. She began telling me of her situation which explained her stressed and somewhat confused state. Anyone else in this situation would feel the same. Apparently, she had to return home to India to have her arm surgically repaired after she broke it ice skating a few weeks back, when she initially came to Canada. Compounding her problems, she had to find a new place to live as her landlord told her she had to find a new home in only two weeks.

She began crying as it was all getting to be too much. As such, I told her I had a lead on a room, and I would get back to her if she was willing to stay in touch. As things transpired, she connected with the landlord, and everything worked out as she is still there! In the following weeks, months, and now years, we have become good friends. As it goes in life, so much has happened since our first encounter. For example, she had an accident that required emergency dental work, she had problems with an unscrupulous co-worker, getting her driver's licence, and her father died. Now, some three years later, she is a Permanent Resident in Canada and has even managed to not only bring her daughter over from India but has opened a new restaurant in the heart of Toronto with a partner!

Sharmi stayed true to her goals and managed to stay focused despite incredible obstacles and barriers. In turn, I learned of the hardships new immigrants and foreign students face as they try to integrate in a new

Country especially with our Indian community! We have remained in constant contact and have become dear friends. Sharmi has my utmost respect for all she has endured and overcome to attain her new status in Canada.

To think I helped, in my own small way, is extremely gratifying!

Driving a bus has afforded me incredible opportunities to help folks, and when I see the results in people such as Sharmi, it brings me an incredible amount of gratification.

All because I drive a bus and am a Bus Driver who cares for people!

How I Became a Bus Driver – by Claude Boucher

I WAS A SUPERVISOR WITH A MAJOR RAILWAY COMPANY IN their Intermodal Division. I fully intended to finish off my career in their Appointments and Dispatch department. Alas, it was not to be as with all big corporations they downsize from time to time, and I became a number and found myself unemployed. Well, here I was at a crossroads. Too young to retire, yet old enough to worry about 'what do I do now at my age?!'

I took about six months to figure things out. Through depression and a lot of self-reflection as to what went wrong and of what to do now?! I started my renewal and self-reflection from within. Questioning my values and qualities in what I liked most about myself. In that I love; playing with big toys, working, and dealing with people, traveling, being outdoors, the flexibility driving for a living affords you, but most of all - I love and care for people!

I will never forget when I was 18, back in the mid-1970's, and took an aptitude test at the YMCA. The test underlined my extremely caring and emotional nature. Their advice was to avoid pursuing a career in teaching or social work. There was a very high likelihood that I would end up hurting myself more than I could help others. The fact that I might drown in others emotional issues and problems might be an issue for all parties involved. However, a good alternative was presented in the form of coaching or assisting people in small doses, in order to keep and maintain that safe, emotional distance.

So, here I am, 55 years old, starting all over again from square one. After my wallowing and depression, I pulled myself up from my bootstraps, as my father used to say, or 'you make your bed as you sleep in it,' as my mother used to say, and began my journey for Claude down Claude's Highway of Life!

Then, it suddenly hit me! To begin a career as a bus driver. It satisfied all my basic needs, and I chartered a course to do just that. I decided to become a Coach bus driver. Never in my wildest dreams did I think I would be a driver in the Urban Transit field. The question still remained, 'how do I get started?'

I saw an ad for school bus drivers. Free training included which would lead to a bus driver's license. That was my first step after wearing a suit to work every day in the railway industry, to driving a little school bus of kindergarten kids in my blossoming new career. I had my foot in the door and was gaining valuable experience with bigger and better buses. I continued to plan my new future. After a few months of driving a school bus, I was accepted and promoted to the larger school buses doing Charter routes. It was invaluable as it led me to where I wanted to be, driving Highway Coach Buses, and traveling with groups and doing tours.

In the beginning, it was awesome and incredible. But the reality and honeymoon period soon wore thin as the hours were incredibly long and the schedule was never stable and being the 'family man' I am, it was simply too much. Having said that, the best time of my life was being selected as the designated driver for The Ryerson Women's Hockey Team (renamed the Toronto Metropolitan University)! Unfortunately, they did not play every day, or I would still be doing that today, no doubt.

I began searching again, but in keeping my new career goals intact. I started to apply to Urban Transit Companies.

I did some research to determine the best fit for me as a person and in relation to where I lived. Taking into consideration their customer service values, training department, initial hiring status (Part-time,

Contract or Full time, etc.,), and wage structure, I gave each a numeric value and determined exactly which company I wanted to work for.

At first, I was accepted by the least of my favourite choices, but I took it just to get my foot in the door to the Urban Transit world. Finally, I had a relatively stable schedule and knew where I would be sleeping every night. I worked for them for a few months and then the call came from my number one choice! Over time, the other major companies contacted me, but I was set as all the pieces of my life began falling into place.

While I feel my employer is simply the best in the region, for corporate and legal issues, I will not disclose the name of the company I work for. Official endorsement of this book on their part might place unrealistic expectations on my fellow drivers, and the company in general.

(Jarry's Smoked Meat - whenever I visit Montreal Canada... my number one treat!)

Honorary Mention

IN WRAPPING UP MY BOOK, I'VE GOT TO GIVE A "SHOUT-out" to all my peers and coworkers who are involved in our "transportation industry" of moving people... including folks in our supervisory, cleaning, maintenance, administration, dispatch, and allocation departments... with special kudos and 'shout-out' to **Simone Smith** (in our Allocation / Dispatch department) and **Ron Johnston** (a fellow Bus Driver and Union Steward in our Garage)! Both never lose sight of the 'human factor' in our day-to-day routines as they are mainstays in keeping our garage running smoothly!

Bus Drivers are an extraordinary group of people! We don't move cargo; we move people to and from their homes or from wherever they may be! Bus drivers are a humble group of mostly caregivers who genuinely care for people! Sure, some may be burned out... no different than many of our passengers, but by far the majority care about people first and foremost!

In fact, each driver can share their own endless stories of unique adventures on their Buses, as I am not alone with my stories! And, when I think of some of our passengers and of how we may have influenced their lives... it is incredibly humbling and rewarding for all of us!

A prime example is Phillipe Vanier who is a Bus driver in Montreal QC, in Canada. Phil is constantly working with and for his peers as a

Bus Driver and Union Steward, and then during his off hours is tirelessly Managing or Coaching kids in Baseball and Hockey!

Thank you for your efforts!

My friends, I'm oh so proud to be a part of your industry!

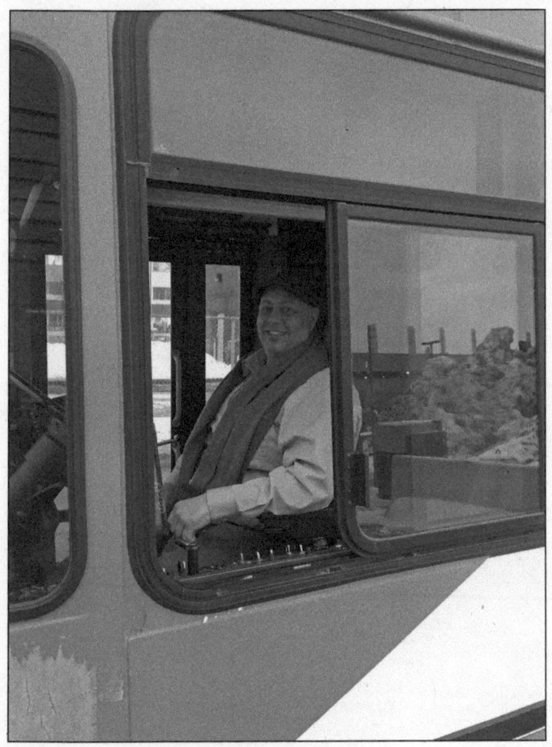

(Philippe Vanier)

Be safe folks,

"Claude, as in Clode the door" …the "French Man raised on Curry" (born in Montreal to a mother from the Caribbean) signing off.

🚍vroom vroom🚍

"Be the pebble thrown into a pond which creates ripples of goodness..."

Printed in Canada